The Rise of India

Its Transformation from Poverty to Prosperity

The Rise of India

Its Transformation from
Poverty to Prosperity

Niranjan Rajadhyaksha

John Wiley & Sons (Asia) Pte Ltd

Copyright © 2007 John Wiley & Sons (Asia) Pte Ltd
Published in 2007 by John Wiley & Sons (Asia) Pte Ltd
2 Clementi Loop, #02-01 Singapore 129809

The publication is designed to provide accurate and authoritative information with regard to the subject matter covered. It is sold with the understanding that the Publisher is not engaged in rendering professional services. If professional advice or other expert assistance is required the services of a competent professional person should be sought.

Other Wiley Editorial Offices
John Wiley & Sons, Inc., 111 River Street, Hoboken, NJ 07030, USA
John Wiley & Sons Ltd, The Atrium, Southern Gate, Chichester PO19 BSQ, England
John Wiley & Sons (Canada) Ltd, 5353 Dundas Street West, Suite 400, Toronto, Ontariao M9B 6H8, Canada
John Wiley & Sons Australia Ltd, 42 McDougall Street, Milton, Queensland 4064, Australia
Wiley-VCH, Boschstrasse 12, D-69469 Weinheim, Germany

Library of Congress Cataloging-in-Publication Data:
ISBN-13 978-0-470-82201-2
ISBN-10 0-470-82201-5

Typeset in 11/13 points Sabon by Gantech

Printed in Singapore by Saik Wah Press Pte Ltd.
10 9 8 7 6 5 4 3 2 1

For my parents

Contents

Acknowledgments. ix

Introduction. 1

Chapter 1: Fear Over the Valley. 11

Chapter 2: A Century of Lost Opportunities 29

Chapter 3: People Power 49

Chapter 4: India Calling. 67

Chapter 5: The Global Agenda 85

Chapter 6: The Financial Revolution 103

Chapter 7: The Yogi and the Consumer. 121

Chapter 8: Reforms for the Poor: The Acid Test 133

Chapter 9: The Dark Side of the Moon 151

Epilogue. 167

Index 173

Acknowledgments

One of the advantages of being a journalist is that you get to meet so many people — influential people, interesting people, and (very occasionally) influential people who are also interesting. It is now more than seventeen years since I decided to quit teaching economics to undergraduates and start writing about it for a wider audience. Over this period, I have been lucky to meet a wide variety of people — from company CEOs and central bank governors to rural artisans and struggling entrepreneurs. The list of those who have been kind enough to share their experiences and views with me is too long to put down here. All I can do here is (to borrow a smart phrase from the world of blogging) give a hat-tip to all of them.

There are also many others to thank. The core ideas in this book have been discussed and debated over with many close friends, especially Philip George, Kumar Ketkar, Shrirang Purohit, Aniruddha Phadke, Girish Naravane, Aneesh Pradhan, Indrajit Gupta, T. Surendar, Shishir Prasad, N. Sriram, Niraj Bhatt, Mehul Bhatt, Avinash Celestine, and M. Rajshekhar. A few economist friends too have always been ready to talk to me about what has been happening in the Indian economy: Narendra Jadhav, S.S. Bhandare, Mahesh Vyas, Ajit Ranade, Rupa Rege-Nitsure, Avinash Paranjape, and Chandrahas Deshpande. At *Business World* magazine, I have been lucky to work with Parthasarthi Swami, T.N. Ninan, and Tony Joseph, three editors who unfailingly encouraged me to write on the issues that interested me. Two other senior colleagues — Prosenjit Dutta and D.N. Mukherjea — were kind enough to carry the extra burden in the office when I was away writing this book. Sheril Dias has kept a semblance of order in my office for nearly a decade, despite my best efforts to do otherwise.

There is no doubt in my mind that this book would not have seen the light of day without the active encouragement of Nick Wallwork and Janis Soo. My friend and editor Sharadchandra Panse knocked off many errors, both factual and grammatical, from the initial manuscript. The errors that still linger on are my responsibility.

There are a few other personal debts to be acknowledged. The talented team that worked in the Mumbai office of *Business World* magazine between 2000 and 2005 was a great combination of professional ability and personal friendships, and I owe a lot to every member of that team. My childhood friend Dr Kaustubh Vaidya and our family physician Dr P.R. Deshpande saw me through a potentially serious health problem. For no reason specifically connected to this book but for a hundred other reasons, the all-important circle of friends at Sahitya Sahawas, a wonderful housing colony in Mumbai which was set up by a group of writers and critics nearly 40 years ago and where we all grew up; life would just not be the same without these childhood friends. I wrote large parts of this book in an office of Baysquare Technologies, a telecom software firm set up by four of my friends. There, Satyajit Kanekar and Shaunak Joshi kept me going by supplying tea, playing music and talking about cricket whenever mental fatigue set in. Avinash Gowarikar, who is usually busy taking photographs of glamorous movie stars, had to deal with a far more prosaic model for this book.

Nothing would have been possible without my family. A big thanks to my parents and my sisters for everything they have done for me over the years. And, finally, a personal note to Sayali, my wife, and to Saawani and Sharvari, my little daughters. To them, I say (with some relief): "The book is finally done. Now you can once again take charge of the computer at home to play games, do your homework, chat, and listen to music. It is all yours!"

Introduction

I suppose it is a bit odd to start a book on the Indian economy with a quote from *Playboy* magazine, but I will run the risk nevertheless. In March 1977, the magazine that is famous for its cerebral approach to life published an interview with Daniel Patrick Moynihan. He had been US ambassador to India during the Nixon administration and then had had a stint as US Permanent Representative to the United Nations during Gerald Ford's presidency. When the interview was published, Moynihan was set for a long and distinguished tenure in the US Senate.

The interviewer asked Moynihan about US policy on India, which had been in the midst of an unusual two-year hiatus from democracy and free speech — the Emergency — when the interview was taped. Moynihan's answer was blunt:

> "While the second most populous nation in the world was a democracy, the United States had an enormous ideological interest in the prosperity and success of that country. We want the world to know that democracies do well. So they've given up on the one claim they had on us. When India ceased to be a democracy, our actual interest there just plummeted. I mean, what does it export but communicable disease?"[1]

Moynihan's answer to the interviewer was infuriating — for an Indian at any rate — but also interesting in equal measure. That bit about the United States having an "enormous ideological interest" in the prosperity and success of India was more rhetoric than reality. The "natural alliance of democracies" was most often little more than an empty slogan during the Cold War. The United States was quite prepared to shake hands with tyrants of all sorts as long as they were ready to join its camp. A little over five years earlier, in the winter of 1971, democratic India had gone to war with a Pakistan under military rule. The fight had erupted because of the butchery that the Pakistani army had unleashed in the former East Pakistan, which was to emerge as the independent nation of

Bangladesh after the war. The United States had then sided with the Pakistani dictators and even sent part of its naval fleet into the Indian Ocean to pressure India. So Moynihan's grand posturing about the natural friendship between democracies has to be taken with a pinch of salt.

However, it is the last line of his blunt answer that is really interesting. The question whether India exported anything other than communicable disease touched upon a disturbing truth. India actually did not export anything of note in 1977. It was neither a big importer nor a big exporter, which was not surprising considering the fact that foreign trade was looked upon with suspicion in those years. Self-sufficiency was the magic mantra. Nor was India a magnet for foreign investment. Moynihan had touched upon the stark fact that an economic weakling asleep in a cocoon would not be taken seriously by the rest of the world. And — let us face it — India *was* an economic weakling in the 1970s.

INDIA STARTS TO RECLAIM ITS LOST POSITION

Nearly 30 years after Moynihan's interview to *Playboy*, there has been a dramatic change in the situation. The country that he so imperiously dismissed as exporting "… [nothing] but communicable disease" is being assiduously wooed by governments and corporations from around the world. Why? Because India's economic performance has finally begun to match its economic potential. The Indian economy has been one of the fastest-growing economies of the world over the past quarter-century. This book tries to explain what is driving India's remarkable economic transformation — something that could finally help its billion and more citizens break out of the shackles imposed by centuries of mass poverty.

India was once a premier economic power. The wealth of the Indies was the stuff of commercial folklore in Europe in the 16th and 17th centuries. It was this wealth that attracted successive waves of traders and conquerors. In the period between 1500 and 1700, the years when Europe started crawling out of its stagnant Dark Ages and into the bright light of the Renaissance and the Industrial Revolution, India accounted for about a quarter of the world's output.[2] Its share started declining after the early 19th century, gradually at first, then precipitously. In 1950, just three years after India emerged as an independent nation, India's share of global GDP was down to a mere 4.17%. It was only in the 1990s that India, for the first time in nearly 300 years, saw its share of world output climb, because it was only then that it began taking the first tentative steps that could put it back on the long journey to prosperity and enable it to reclaim a share of global GDP that is more in line with the size of its population (Table 1).

Table 1
India's Share of World Economy (%)

Year	1500	1600	1700	1820	1900	1950	1990	2000
Share	24.36	22.43	24.44	16.02	8.6	4.17	4.05	5.27

Source: Angus Maddison.

India lost its way after the 18th century for a variety of reasons and is now preparing to reoccupy its rightful position in the world economy. Its emergence from poverty and destitution will change the rest of the world in myriad ways, just as China's stunning attack on poverty since 1979 has. For example, India's rapid economic growth is likely to keep a lid on wages in the rich countries, take the lid off global energy prices, and fundamentally change the balance of economic power in the world. The march of a billion people out of poverty and into some modicum of prosperity is bound to send ripples (and an occasional shock wave) into the rest of the world.

BUT HAVE WE NOT HEARD THIS BEFORE?

This is neither the first book on India's economic boom and nor, of course, will it be the last. However, I believe (and hope) that *The Rise of India* will not be a complete waste of a reader's time, for reasons I will presently explain.

The recent spate of books and reports that have dealt with how various policies have helped and hindered economic growth in India can fill up several library shelves. It is not my intention to add to the pile. There have been endless debates in India on globalization, the need for foreign investment, the quest for a more balanced budget, or rational tax policy. I have more or less steered clear of these debates. There is no attempt here to deny the role of sensible economic policies in promoting growth. India has suffered for too long from muddled or plain bad economic policies; so the converse can well be taken as proven true from the very start: policies that promote enterprise and hard work are a fundamental requirement in an economy striving for efficiency and prosperity. I have no major quarrels with the mainstream view that India needs a smaller fiscal deficit, a national value-added tax, low inflation, more privatization, a less regulated economy, etc.

However, neither economic growth nor economic policies are ends in themselves. It is people who create wealth, not governments. Economic policy is the structuring of incentives and disincentives in the economy. It is *how* individuals and organizations *respond to* these incentives and disincentives that determines economic performance. In a paper (now lost) he read to the Glasgow Club in 1755, Adam Smith is believed to have said:

> "Little else is requisite to carry a state to the highest degree of opulence from the lowest barbarism, but peace, easy taxes, and a tolerable administration of justice; all the rest being brought about by the natural course of things. All governments that thwart this natural course, which force things into another channel, or which endeavour to arrest the progress of society at a particular point, are unnatural, and to support themselves are obliged to be oppressive and tyrannical."

Modern-day governments do have to do more things than the bare three that Smith talked about that day in Glasgow. Anyway, Smith said these words more than two decades before he wrote his classic, *An Inquiry into the Nature and Causes of the Wealth of Nations*, in 1776. By then Smith himself was perhaps ready to accept that government needed to do more than maintain peace, keep taxes low, and administer justice. Yet, his more general point continues to be an attractive one. If governments do a few things right, prosperity will follow "by the natural course of things." I imagine Smith did not mean that opulence would follow automatically, but merely that it would be a natural consequence of good policies.

History tells us that when people are empowered with basic economic rights, they can turn dust into diamonds. Policy changes can help or hinder this process; but it is people and their commercial organizations that are the real stars of an economic transformation. It is the job of a journalist to track these stars. My trade has allowed me to examine the changes that have taken place in the factory, on the street and in the bazaar. This book is not about monetary aggregates or trade policies; it is about companies that are coming to terms with globalization, fishermen using mobile phones to maximize their revenues, parents striving to get their children to school, farmers trying to link to modern markets and young people aspiring to move up in life. In other words, it is an attempt to examine what Adam Smith called the "natural course of things."

DEVELOPMENT IS CHOICE

Economic growth should not be confused with economic development. The latter has been defined variously. My personal preference is the definition put forward by Peter Bauer, one of the few development economists in the second half of the 20th century with a classical liberal bent of mind. In 1957, Bauer wrote:

> "I regard the extension of the range of choice, that is, an increase in the range of effective alternatives open to people, as the principal objective and criterion of economic development; and I judge a measure principally by its probable effects on the range of alternatives open to individuals.... My position is much influenced by my dislike of policies or measures which are likely to increase man's power over man; that is, to increase the control of groups or individuals over the fellow men."[3]

Bauer's definition of economic development is typically succinct and clear-headed. It is easy to get drawn deep into macroeconomic numbers, elegant mathematical models, and heated ideological battles. They are not unimportant. Yet, the reference point of economic debate, policy, and performance should be the increase in freedom and choice for individuals. This is not just about choosing between five types of cars, 50 types of shoes or a 100 television channels. Consumer choice is a small subset of the larger universe of choice. It is about the ability of a poor farm worker to choose between ill health and good health; the range of career options open to a bright student; and the power available to a fisherman to decide in which market to sell his catch. That is what economic development is actually about, rather than the quarterly GDP numbers that economists and financial markets are so enticed by.

In short, this book is about how the economic transformation of the world's second most populous nation and largest democracy is helping millions of its people benefit from freedom and choice.

THE SIX GREAT REVOLUTIONS

The story of India's phoenix-like rise from the economic ashes can be told in many ways. The way I have preferred to tell it is as follows. Six great revolutions are changing the very nature of Indian economy and society. The progress of these revolutions has been uneven; some have been wildly successful while others have been progressing in fits and starts. Here is a quick overview.

The Demographic Revolution: India is a young country in an aging world. It is rapidly moving toward a demographic sweet spot, when the share of people of working age in the total population will peak. Fewer dependents will mean, among other things, higher rates of savings, investment, and growth.

The Globalization Revolution: Of all the economic mistakes that India made after Independence, perhaps none was more serious than the decision to withdraw into a protectionist shell. Now, higher levels of trade and investments across national borders are helping Indians specialize, forcing them to be more productive, and giving them access to technological and organizational knowledge.

The Outsourcing Revolution: The drop in telecom costs and the increasing digitization of key processes has helped global companies transfer parts of their value chain to India, home to a huge pool of cheap and effective manpower. What started off at the lowend of the value chain (like fielding calls from dissatisfied credit card users in the West) has now spread to more high-value work like chip design or pharmaceutical research.

The Financing Revolution: India's savings rate has started climbing. It is the job of the financial sector to ensure that these savings are channeled into the right sectors and projects. While Indian banks are more stable than many of their Asian counterparts, they have not been able to reach out to the people who really need bank loans. The move toward greater financial inclusion has now begun.

The Aspirations Revolution: Twenty-five years of strong economic growth and 15 years of exposure to the world — be it through trade, tourism or cable television — have unleashed a wave of social change in India. It is very difficult to precisely define the contours of this wave. But there is no missing it: the new generation expects a better life and is not ashamed to pursue it.

The Policy Revolution: Many of the old shibboleths of economic policy have now been buried, but not all of them. The poor still find it difficult to participate in and benefit from the global economy. Another round of reforms is needed to address this problem. It means far-reaching changes — from freeing markets to building roads. But the most important challenge: giving property rights and access to finance to the poor. This is one of the biggest unfinished tasks in India.

Each trend — naturally — comes embedded with certain problems and ensuring that these problems are dealt with satisfactorily will test the resilience and creativity of Indian society. For example, a young population can be a blessing only if the millions of potential workers are educated and skilled and have jobs to use their knowledge and skills. Otherwise, there will be growing hopelessness and frustration. The vitality that is bubbling up to the surface today can quickly transform itself into rage.

CERTAINTIES AND PROBABILITIES

To paraphrase what the philosopher J. Krishnamurthi said about Truth, the future is a pathless land. We can never be completely sure what will happen tomorrow. Karl Popper warned us to doubt all views based on pseudo-scientific theories of historical inevitability. Futures can at best be explained in terms of their probabilities. There is a very high probability that the Indian economic miracle is here to stay for a few decades. But it is not a certainty. Nothing ever is.

One of the perils of journalism is being forced to hear self-appointed experts divine the future with absolute certainty — stock pickers who pretend to identify sure winners, management gurus who tell companies what the road ahead looks like, tech gurus who lecture on what products will capture our attention next year and (let it also be said) journalists who hold forth on the future with utter confidence. This book tries to stay away from such a whirlpool of certitudes.

India has just taken the first few steps on the road to prosperity. It is still a poor country and has a long way to go before it can even reach the levels of development seen in a Thailand or an Argentina.

The road ahead is bound to have bumps on the way — economic, social, and political. Even as I was writing this book in the first quarter of 2006, there were clear signs that there was a bubble building up in the domestic equity market and that the current account deficit was growing at a worrisome pace (as the book was in the process of going to press, the bubble burst and the equity market plummeted).

In the last few weeks of the previous year, armed Maoist rebels had stormed a prison in the northern state of Bihar to free their comrades; and for a short time helped focus attention on how desperately poor some regions of the country still are. The threats posed by divisive politics based on caste, religion, and region should never be underestimated in as complex a country as India.

India's long march out of poverty is unlikely to be a smooth one. Yet, what is important is that Indians — one out of every six people on the planet — now have a better chance than ever to break the shackles imposed by centuries of poverty and economic inertia. The rest of the world is watching their progress — as well as the threats, risks, and opportunities that the rise of India will throw up.

NOTES

1. *The Playboy Interview* edited by G. Barry Golson, New York: Playboy Press, 1981, p.509.
2. Available at: http://www.ggdc.net/maddison/, the home page of Angus Maddison.
3. P.T. Bauer, *Economic Analysis And Policy In Underdeveloped Countries*, Greenwood Press Reprint, 1981.

Let New India arise — out of the peasants' cottage, grasping the plough; out of the huts of the fisherman, the cobbler and the sweeper. Let her spring from the shop, from beside the oven of the fritter seller. Let her emanate from the factory, from marts and from markets. Let her emerge from groves and forests, from hills and mountains.

—Swami Vivekananda

Chapter 1

Fear Over the Valley

A new word appeared on the fringes of the English language sometime at the end of 2003. Anxious technology workers in Silicon Valley were seen sporting it on T-shirts that said: *I have been Bangalored*. The word "Bangalored" captured the fear of the moment. Silicon Valley was barely recovering from the painful dot-com bust of 2001, though dark clouds of doubt still hovered over an area that was, till recently, known for its sunny optimism. Engineers and code writers in Silicon Valley, and in many other parts of the rich world, were worried that they would lose their jobs to cheaper labor in Bangalore, a charming city in south India that has emerged as the country's technology hub. Across the Atlantic Ocean, in the United Kingdom, a variant of the anti-outsourcing T-shirt was available with a plainer message: *My Job Went To India — And All I Got Was This Lousy T-shirt*.

Of course, there was an element of irony in these sartorial protests. The US T-shirts were being sold by an anti-outsourcing website at a pricey $15.99. Soon, there were jokes about them in Internet chat rooms visited by Indian technology workers. The standard quip went something like this: *Those T-shirts are way too expensive; the anti-outsourcing brigade should have reduced costs by outsourcing their production to India*. The point of all this good-natured banter was that the economics of outsourcing is too compelling to be ignored in a global economy built on the hard realities of comparative advantage.

More than two billion Indians and Chinese have become participants in the global economy. Their entry into the global labor market is bound to push down wages in many industries and rewrite the economics in many sectors of the modern economy. China had already packed malls in cities from Los Angeles to

Tokyo with its cheap consumer goods. India was threatening to do something similar with its cheap services. These were likely to be the first rumblings of a tectonic shift in global economic power.

THE BATTLE LINES ARE DRAWN

Outsourcing stirred up a massive controversy in the United States and Europe at the dawn of the new century. TV host Lou Dobbs, who has a show every weeknight on CNN, ran a controversial series called Exporting America, in which he featured US companies outsourcing jobs to places like Bangalore. John Kerry, the Democratic Party's candidate in the 2004 US presidential election, made the issue a core part of his election platform. "We will repeal every single benefit, every single loophole, every single reward for any Benedict Arnold CEO or corporation that take American jobs overseas and stick you with the bill," he thundered in a speech given on February 10, 2004 in Virginia.[1] (Benedict Arnold was a general in the American army during the War of Independence against the British who later collaborated with the enemy.)

N. Gregory Mankiw, then chairman of the US president's Council of Economic Advisors, had to face the heat from irate politicians for his insistence that the outsourcing of everything from software design to low-end accounting work was just a new form of international trade. It would bring along all the attendant benefits that come with specialization and division of labor. He said in the course of a press briefing:

> "Outsourcing is just a way of doing international trade. We're very used to goods being produced abroad and being shipped here on ships or planes. What we're not very used to is services being produced abroad and being sent here over the Internet or telephone wires. But does it matter from an economic standpoint whether items produced come on planes and ships or over fiber optic cables? Well, no; the economics is basically the same. More things are tradable than were tradable in the past, and that's a good thing."[2]

Many eminent economists quickly came out in support of Mankiw. Among them was Jagdish Bhagwati, perhaps the world's foremost trade theorist and for long an ardent supporter of free trade between nations. But there was opposition that went beyond the soapbox oratory of television hosts and presidential candidates. No less a person that Paul Samuelson, *eminence grise* of modern economics, criticized Mankiw and Bhagwati. Samuelson said in an academic paper that he thought the likes of Bhagwati and Mankiw were the perpetrators of "the popular polemical untruth."[3] Mankiw later wrote: "During the presidential campaign of 2004, no economic issue generated more heat or shed less light than the debate over offshore outsourcing."[4]

Meanwhile, some countries tried to get around the challenge by importing workers rather than exporting jobs. The United States and the United Kingdom have traditionally had relatively liberal immigration laws. In 2000, the German federal government tried to introduce a law that would allow skilled workers — especially computer programmers from India — to come in as temporary citizens through a system of Green Cards for guest workers. Protests erupted in no time. One of the more combative slogans said: *Kinder Statt Inder* (have children, instead of letting in Indians).

Indians did not know what to make of this sudden attention. They were more used to striking pity rather than fear in cities like San Francisco, Berlin, and London. Ironically, one thing that the vocal opponents of outsourcing never quite figured out is that their loud protests actually helped the "villains" in India. I remember meeting the head of one of India's top software companies for breakfast around the time that Lou Dobbs was carrying on his television campaign. What this CEO told me was interesting. He said that till the controversies made it to prime time, only the very large US corporations were aware of the real benefits of outsourcing. Now, he told me, even the smaller companies in the corporate version of Middle America were being told day in and day out how sending part of their work to India could save costs. They too jumped onto the bandwagon. The outsourcing market actually increased because its opponents were impractical enough to cast the spotlight on it. They were the unwitting and unlikely ambassadors of outsourcing.

OUTSOURCING AND BEYOND

The sabre-rattling ended soon after the T-shirts and the TV shows. The Bush administration had started cutting taxes after 2002. The budget surpluses of the Clinton years were to make way for yawning deficits in America. The US Federal Reserve too cut interest rates. This huge stimulus package — while creating other problems like a bubble in housing prices and a $500 billion current account deficit — ensured that the first recession of the 21st century was a tolerably short one. There were initial fears that the economic recovery would be a jobless one. It was many months into the recovery before new jobs were created in the United States. (Many European countries continue to suffer from high levels of structural unemployment.) This was at about the same time when the paranoia about being "Bangalored" peaked — at least in the United States. As hiring picked up, the fears about outsourcing to India died down.

Two years later, millions of people around the world were commuting to work armed with the iconic gadget of our times, the Apple iPod. (Perhaps even Lou Dobbs has one.) Few seemed to know — or care — that the brain of the digital music player is partly made in India. The chip that powers the iPod is made by a company called Portal Player, headquartered in Santa Clara, California. Part of its chip-design work is done in the Indian city of Hyderabad, where Portal Player has a subsidiary. About half the company's employees work in the Hyderabad facility. To some, the iPod is a miniature representation of the new global economy.

An article by Andrew Leonard in *Der Spiegel* talks about "a golden triangle new world order in which every nation contributes what it does best — low-cost development in India, manufacturing in China, high-level design in the United States — and all prosper together."[5] An estimated 150 top global companies had moved part of their research and development work to India by the end of 2005. The list includes giants like Microsoft, Intel, and Nokia. Many of them came to save costs but are now investing to take advantage of India's intellectual skills. "We came to India for the costs, we stayed for the quality, and we're now investing for the innovation," Dan Scheinman, senior vice-president for corporate development at Cisco Systems told *Business Week* magazine.[6]

India has also muscled its way into the business plans of many companies. A few have even held their board meetings in India — for example, HSBC, Nokia, Siemens, and Perot Systems. While the achievements of its technology companies continued to dominate the headlines across the world, there were other attractive features in India that have gradually caught attention — its huge domestic consumer market, its telecom revolution, the first attempts to repair its tattered infrastructure. India is now regularly mentioned in the same breath as China in articles and conferences. Raghuram Rajan, economic counselor and director of the research department at the International Monetary Fund, pointed out in a speech he made to an audience of global Indians that the Western press these days rarely mentions China without adding "and India."[7]

THE SIGNIFICANCE OF THE OUTSOURCING DEBATES

So was that outsourcing furore of 2004 "full of sound and fury, signifying nothing?" No, it was not. Sceptics have been quick to point out that despite all the attention lavished on India's technology companies, they constitute a thin slice of the larger economic cake. A few tech hotspots are unlikely to matter much in a country that is as large as India. There is little doubt that India's technology services companies, for all their success, are a tiny part of the overall economy in terms of output and employment. Yet, there are several reasons why the success of India's outsourcing industry and the debates it stirred up should be considered momentous events.

The controversies marked the first time in modern history that India's economic prowess was seen as a threat by the rest of the world. The country of rajas, gurus, tigers, and emaciated peasants was suddenly seen as something more — an emerging economic and technological powerhouse. Even the Chinese asked enviously — what do we learn from India's success in software exports? Though millions of Indians continue to live in appalling poverty and battle hunger every night, the world realized that there was a glimmer of hope in the world's second most populous nation and largest democracy. And this was why the polemical battles about the export of jobs to India are important. They cast the spotlight on the rise of India.

A CAUTIONARY TALE

With a quarter of its population battling extreme poverty, the last thing India needs is premature celebrations or bouts of overconfidence. Its recent successes are a tentative beginning rather than a grand finale. Economic history is littered with many examples of countries that have belied their initial promise — just as, in the stock market, we remember the handful of winners and conveniently forget the many dud stocks that showed early promise. Those who believe that there is a touch of inevitability to India's journey out of poverty would do well to remember this sobering lesson. Let's look at countries that lost their way after a good start. Many Europeans looked to Argentina as an escape from the scarcity-ridden realities of post-war Europe. Brazil was the toast of the development crowd in the 1950s and 1960s. Indonesia could do no wrong in the eyes of the financial herd till the Asian crisis of 1997 sent its economy into a tailspin. On the other hand, in the early years after World War II, Japan was often dismissed as an overcrowded and resource-poor island. And few would care to remember the chaos in China during Mao's years of senility.

In 1964, Joan Robinson, one of the finest economists of the post-war era and a member of John Maynard Keynes' inner circle at Cambridge, wrote this about Korea: "All economic miracles of the postwar world are put in shade by these achievements."[8] The trouble was that she was writing about North Korea, Kim Il Sung's madcap socialist utopia that would be on the brink of mass starvation by the 1990s after it stopped getting subsidies from the Soviet Union. It's not that Robinson was a lone voice as far as North Korea's economic future went. Many others also believed that it had a brighter future than South Korea, that its hermetic economic nationalism was superior to the corrupt policies of the military dictatorship ruling in Seoul. Joan Robinson was not t0he only one to get it wrong. In 1960, some 450,000 Koreans living in Japan officially selected North Korea as their "mother country." Only 165,000 selected South Korea. Between 1959 and 1962, around 75,000 Koreans left Japan and settled in the communist North.

The moral of these stories is that economic futures are not unalterable. There will always be surprises along the road, both nasty and pleasant. Many countries stumble along the way; some pick themselves up, while others languish by the roadside. Parallel examples can be found in the rich world as well. Japan and Germany were widely regarded as unstoppable winners in the 1980s and beyond — perpetual miracle machines that would dominate the global economy. There were books galore on how the rest of the world should learn from these two countries. As it happened, Japan spent most of the 1990s in recession, while Germany struggled with low growth.

India too has had false starts before. There was a lot going for it when it started off on the path of planned economic development in the 1950s — a modern leadership, a strong civil service, and a diversified industrial base, for instance. Many of the world's top economists (like Nicholas Kaldor, Oscar Lange, and Michael Kalecki) were brought in as advisors to design independent India's growth strategy. Economic management too was prudent. The government did not run up crippling deficits and debt. Inflation rarely went over 20%, at a time when many other developing countries (this is before they were cleverly rebranded as emerging markets) had to suffer hyper-inflation. There were political storms every time the inflation rate came close to 20%. And a democratic political system ensured that India was spared the insane upheavals such as the Great Leap Forward and the Cultural Revolution that China had to endure.

Yet, the economy was sluggish after an initial burst of growth. The fifteen years after 1965 were a period of listless and apathetic economic performance. Meanwhile, a string of Asian countries broke through their poverty traps with the help of miraculous rates of growth. First it was Japan, then the four original tiger economies of Hong Kong, Singapore, Taiwan, and South Korea. Others like Thailand, Malaysia, and Indonesia followed. Each of these countries had two decades or more of economic growth in excess of 8%. India hobbled along at around 3.5% a year, which meant that economic growth barely kept pace with population growth. Incomes almost stagnated.

To switch metaphors, the successive economic miracles in Asia are sometimes compared to a formation of flying geese. One goose leads the flight. The others follow in a V-shaped pattern. Japan was that initial flying goose for many Asian countries. In the three decades after it was virtually razed to the ground in the Second World War, Japan's economy soared at breakneck speed. It created a beautiful arc of economic success in East Asia. The others followed its flight path. Even China joined after 1979. India preferred to remain rooted to the ground, content with the modest pickings there. Its goose, so to say, was cooked.

A MALTHUSIAN SCARE

There was even a time when India was dismissed as a hopeless case. It seemed to be sitting on a Malthusian time bomb in the late

1960s, as population threatened to grow faster than food supply. The devastating drought of 1966 had brought millions to the brink of starvation. The economy had stalled, the rupee had to be devalued sharply, urban unemployment was severe and Maoist rebels were leading a bloody insurrection in some parts of the country.

Food aid saved the day, but India's economic future seemed bleak. Sharad Pawar, now India's agriculture minister, had joined the state ministry in the western state of Maharashtra in 1972, which was yet another year when the rains had failed. One of his responsibilities was the department of civil supplies. Pawar called in his senior bureaucrats to assess the situation. He was told that they would wait patiently every day for ships laden with food to come from Australia. The food was unloaded and sent into the interior. Most of Pawar's time was spent at the Mumbai port, checking whether the emergency supplies were being unloaded fast enough. India seemed condemned to struggle along with a ship-to-mouth economy.[9]

Was the effort to save India's millions worth it? In 1967, William and Paul Paddock wrote a controversial book: *Famine 1975!* Their thesis was a chilling one. The world was headed for a famine and the United States would do well to use food aid judiciously. The Paddocks argued that food aid to some countries would be self-defeating, since it would act as an incentive for their populations to grow faster. The US government was advised to let people starve rather than feed the Malthusian monster. One country mentioned in this controversial book as a candidate for starvation was India.

The Paddocks were borrowing an idea from the First World War. The brutal trench warfare across Europe had left millions injured. Medical supplies were scarce. Doctors in the Allied medical tents decided to divide the injured into three categories. The first were those who would live even without any medical help. The second were those who would die despite the best care. And the third were those injured soldiers who could be saved with medicines and care. The doctors decided to use their limited supplies to help those in the third category — the wounded men who could be saved with proper medicines and care. The other soldiers were left to live or die on their own. It was more prudent, according to the Paddocks, to let India starve rather than waste scarce food on it. The Swedish economist Gunnar Myrdal attacked all policies based on concepts of "economic triage" in his Nobel Prize acceptance speech in 1976.

He quoted an article in *The New York Times* that called the triage theory "one of the most pessimistic and morally threadbare intellectual positions to be advanced since the demise of the Third Reich."[10] Myrdal and others of his ilk need not have worried. India survived, while the cold-blooded advice to let it starve did not.

The Indian government, which had neglected agriculture in its early development plans, partly based on the old Soviet belief that the future was in steel plants rather than rice farms, saw its mistake. New hybrid seeds were imported from Mexico, banks were forced to lend to farmers and price incentives were put in place. India's farmers responded magnificently, and the country became self-sufficient in foodgrains within five years. This was the country's Green Revolution. There were severe droughts in 1973 and 1987 as well. There was high inflation in both these years, but the specter of mass starvation never threatened India again.

But let us not forget that it was a close thing. India has flirted with mass starvation in the 1960s and Latin-American style bankruptcy in 1990–1991. There will be other scares along the way — political, social, and economic. India will have to overcome many obstacles and climb a few steep hills before it can offer a decent life to all its billion-plus citizens. This little excursion into history will, it is to be hoped, act like a cold splash of water on the face of those who have been intoxicated by India's recent growth record.

POTHOLES AND PERCEPTIONS

First impressions are very important. And the average international traveler's first impression of India is inevitably negative. The airports are a sorry mess, the queues at the immigration counter are too long, the road into town is scarred with potholes and urban poverty is on open display in the slums that line the roads. It is not uncommon to hear one of our modern road-warriors exclaim in exasperation: "Look at China!"

The exasperation is not completely unfounded. My first visit to China left me wide-eyed. I suppose it happens to a lot of Indians when they first set foot in Shanghai or Beijing. Even as my taxi sped along the eight-lane highway from the airport in Shanghai to the new business district at Pudong, I was making quick comparisons with what a similar ride in Mumbai, the city I live in, would entail — potholed roads, slow-moving traffic, and slums on either side. And Pudong did not seem to belong to a country where average incomes were still below $1,000.

The point is that Pudong, though it is undoubtedly an impressive piece of work, is a showpiece rather than a true representation of China.

My reaction to the investment banker haughtily lecturing the Indian government after his first 24 hours in the country is often an offer — to take him into one of the many slums in Mumbai that have recently disturbed his sense of aesthetics. There is poverty here, but also a sense of hope and ambition. He could see vibrant communities, where parents go to work in the morning, children go to school and there is cable TV in most homes. It is the same in other parts of India. There is poverty and squalor, but also hope and progress. There have been changes that are often hidden from the jet-lagged traveler on his way to his five-star hotel.

One of the rare exceptions to this rule was a US diplomat. He told me that he had been to slums in many countries in Africa and Latin America. What he often saw there was crime and despair, drugs, and urban gangs. A Mumbai slum, he told me, exudes energy and confidence. It was quite unlike what he saw in the poor areas of Rio or Lagos or even New York. This man had never actually visited a slum. He too was sitting in a five-star hotel on his first day in India. But he had merely taken the trouble to look beyond the obvious from his car window. I thought this American diplomat — my unconfirmed belief was that he was a Central Intelligence Agency (CIA) man — was remarkably observant.

On my second day in China, I followed my reporter's instinct and left Pudong to visit the old Shanghai across the Huangpu River. It was a world away from the mini-Manhattan in Pudong that hosts the world's business elite. I got myself invited to the house of a man whom I met on the street where he was trying to sell fake Rolex watches. He wanted me to take a look at a wide range of fakes and I wanted to see how he lived. It was a small one-room tenement that he shared with his brother. Their worldly possessions seemed to consist of one large bed, an old cupboard, and a TV that sat in the corner of the small room. They sent part of their earnings back to their parents in the village. It was not very different from what you would find in many Indian cities. The glittering towers of Pudong seemed a world away. A couple of years later, on a train from Hong Kong to Guangzhou, I could see villages and small towns that seemed as poor and chaotic as any in India.

The reason why I am dwelling on my visits to China at such length is simple. We Indians are obsessed with China's success. The remarkable economic transformation there has helped focus the Indian mind on lost possibilities. The two countries were broadly at the same level in 1990. China's levels of health and education were better, but incomes were comparable. Fifteen years later, China's per capita income is twice that of India. Its social and physical infrastructure is leagues ahead. This has led to a strange mix of awe and paranoia. The government wants to match China's growth record. Cities want to model themselves on Shanghai. Companies want to set up factories in China. The newspapers are full of articles on India versus China. Entire seminar seasons across the country have been dedicated to China. This whole India and China thing has become a bit of a tiresome charade.

THE DRAGON AND THE ELEPHANT

The Indian economy is actually quite unlike the Chinese economy, but a closer look at the differences between the two countries helps us understand the Indian economy with greater clarity. Much is made of the fact that India and China have different political systems. India is a thriving, though slightly chaotic, democracy. China is an authoritarian one-party state. A lot of the popular comparisons between India and China revolve around this one fact.

The Nobel Laureate economist Amartya Sen has often said that because of its political structure, independent India has never had to undergo the sort of mass starvation that China did during the Great Leap Forward in the late 1950s. A working democracy and a free press have kept the country free of ridiculous social experiments. But, on the other hand, there are other concerns. Does India's democracy slow down the pace of economic change? There are arduous five-year debates before any decision is taken, be it opening up the insurance sector to foreign investment or laying a modern highway that cuts through a forest. But there is the flipside that often escapes critics. Growth in India can be more sensitive to the needs of the silent majority.

Besides the crucial "democracy versus dictatorship" issue, there are fundamental differences in the economic strategy of the two Asian giants as well. China has mobilized its resources (especially capital) with a single-minded determination. In this, it resembles many other Asian countries whose "economic miracles" were based on input growth rather than productivity. India has been slow in mobilizing resources, but it has used what little it has in a far more efficient manner (note that China uses its female labor force far more than India does, which is perhaps an indication of how important gender rights are for fast development) (Table 2).

Table 2
How The Two Asian Giants Mobilize Inputs

	Labor force participation (as % of population in 15–64 age group)				Gross capital formation (as % of GDP)	
	Male		Female			
	2003	1990	2003	1990	2003	1990
India	88.8	89.6	45.2	42.4	23	26
China	86.6	87.9	79.2	79.9	44.3	36

Source: World Development Indicators 2005, World Bank; DB Research.

A simple calculation can clear some of the obfuscations that damage most popular comparisons between India and China. Since the early 1990s, India has been investing about a quarter of its GDP every year and from this it gets a growth rate of around 6%. So India needs four units of capital to generate one unit of output. China has grown at around 9% a year despite investing nearly half its GDP every year. That means that China needs about five units of capital to get one unit of output. India uses capital more sparingly and efficiently, which is one of the cornerstones of successful capitalism. That is one reason why India has few good roads but many world-class companies. Its economic success is based more on the entrepreneurial energy of its people than on the wisdom of its government.

NETI, NETI

These dichotomies are not uncommon. Alwyn Young of Boston University has compared Singapore and Hong Kong in broadly similar terms. He noted that the two cities were growing at the same rate despite the fact that Singapore had a far higher investment rate. He later expanded his attention to the rest of the region, and found (in Paul Krugman's words) that "Singapore's story of rapid growth achieved through massive growth in inputs rather than growth in efficiency was actually typical of the Asian tigers."[11] In today's context, China is like Singapore while India is like Hong Kong.

China has poured its savings into building new infrastructure and factories. It is an investment story. India has been driven by consumption and productivity. About half of China's national output comes from manufacturing. A similar proportion of India's comes from services. China attracts more than $50 billion of direct foreign investment every year; India manages to attract barely a tenth of that amount. The differences between the two emerging Asian giants pile up. A comparison between the two is, thus, a useful tool to understand the possibilities and perils of the Indian economy with greater clarity.

There is a well-established way of thinking in India. One strand of classical Indian philosophy is based on the principle of negation. The true nature of a thing or a phenomenon can be revealed not by asking what it is but what it is not. An ancient Indian sage was once asked about the nature of the Absolute by his disciples. To each question he answered: "*neti, neti*" (in Sanskrit: *no, no*: that is to say, "not this, not that"). What he was trying to tell his students is that it is easier to know what the Absolute *is not*, rather than what *it is*. So it is perhaps not an accident that India's most significant contribution to modern political action is Mahatma Gandhi's principle of *non*-violence: the *absence* of violence; elsewhere, the preferred expression would probably be passive resistance.

Let's take a look at what India is not, as opposed to China. It's not driven by high investment rates; it does not have an equally strong manufacturing sector; its physical infrastructure is often pathetic; and its dependence on foreign savings is minimal. In many ways, India is what China is not. *Neti, neti*.

THE FUTURE: BRIC BY BRIC

Kishore Mahbubani, former Singapore diplomat and now dean of the Lee Kuan Yew School of Public Policy in the city-state, once wrote about a meeting he had with a young engineer from India. The young man told Mahbubani that Europe would resemble one big museum in the future. People would visit it to see the past. The future was in Asia.

I once asked Mahbubani whether this was unwarranted arrogance. He did not think so. "Yes, arrogance would be a concern. But I think it is better to have pride and confidence than be submissive and fatalistic. I place a lot of emphasis on cultural factors. You cannot succeed unless you believe you can succeed," he told me.[12] The effect of a country's cultural values on its economic performance has always been a bit of a gray area. But there is little doubt that economic growth and cultural confidence are feeding each other in India.

Mahbubani has been a strong votary of Asian values. This school of thought was particularly influential in the 1990s, when the East Asian economies seemed unstoppable. There has been less talk about Asian values since the financial crisis of 1997. While it is always going to be difficult to assess the true impact of culture on economy, public intellectuals like Mahbubani are healthy counterpoints to the old arrogant view that Asian cultures — and especially India's — are incapable of hard work and risk taking.

One may argue with Mahbubani's culture-specific approach, but what matters is that his prediction on the rise of India is no longer like some solitary voice in the wilderness. There are many others, including economists, who talk of India's bright future. On October 26, 2005, Vijay Kelkar, one of India's best economic administrators, delivered the fifth D.R. Gadgil Memorial lecture in Mumbai. Here, he said:

> "We are at the threshold of a golden age of growth, but this historic window of opportunity is available for us only for the next two decades or so. (The) demographic dividend will come to an end as surely and inevitably as the arrow of time. Hence, there is an urgency for us to accelerate reforms."

Earlier, in October 2003, the investment bank Goldman Sachs published a report that proved to be the first in a string of recent research reports on the long-term prospects of the Indian economy — and perhaps the best known.[13] There is a lot that is common in these rosy forecasts. Each of them is based on rigorous forecast models. Each predicts that India's rate of economic growth will move up a few notches in the years ahead. Each says that India will eventually start growing faster than China. And each sees a long-term future when the Indian economy will be bigger than the likes of the United Kingdom, Germany, and Japan (incomes will continue to be modest, however).

Goldman Sachs economists Dominic Wilson and Roopa Purshothaman say that over the next 50 years, what they call the BRIC economies (Brazil, Russia, India, and China) could become a much larger force in the world economy. Of course, they have not merely extrapolated from current growth rates and jumped to their conclusion. Their model takes into account three main factors — population growth, capital accumulation, and productivity growth. Economists will recognize these three building blocks of modern growth theory. Wilson and Purshothaman have then tried to predict the future growth rates of the four emerging giants and those of some of the world's richest economies today. From that, they arrive at estimates for the GDPs of the BRIC countries and the major rich nations of today.

The two Goldman Sachs economists predict that India will overtake Italy in 2015, France in 2020, Germany in 2023, and Japan in 2032. China's economy will be larger than everybody else by 2016 and even larger than the US economy in 2041. Also, they say, "India has the potential to grow the fastest over the next 30 and 50 years." Its GDP growth rate will stay above 5% till 2050; China's will drop to 5% by 2020 and to around 3.5% in the mid-2040s. Or, in other words, the Indian tortoise will eventually outrun the Chinese hare.

This is also what the CIA, among others, thinks. The US National Intelligence Council has what it calls the 2020 Project. It is an attempt to do a bit of crystal ball gazing on global geopolitics in the years ahead. Naturally, economic forecasts are a key part of this study. It too believes that India can sustain its rate of advance longer than China can. Why? The CIA mentions three factors. First, India's working age population will continue to increase well into the 2020s. China's will diminish and age quite rapidly because of its one-child policy. Second, India's democratic institutions make it less vulnerable to political instability. Third, India has well-developed capital markets and world-class firms that will help maintain its long-term competitiveness.

Deutsche Bank is another outfit that is bullish on the India story. In fact, the bank has made the rise of India one of the "mega-themes" of its future research. Deutsche Bank too predicts that India has a rosy future ahead of it. "India will stay on a high growth path of roughly 6% per year on average over the next 10 to 15 years. If reforms are pursued more aggressively, real GDP growth could reach 7–8% a year," says Deutsche Bank economist Jennifer

Asuncion-Mund.[14] She predicts that India will emerge as the fastest of the 34 major emerging markets over the next decade and a half. Its per capita GDP (based on purchasing power parity) will double — from the current $2,500 to $5,000.

> "Within 25 years, India will become one of the world's largest economies. Her growth will be fuelled by superior demographics and rising levels of domestic investment whose power is accentuated by thorough continued economic liberalization. By 2020 India will surpass China as the world's fastest growing major economy and in the process begin to change the world balance of power" (writes Keystone India chief economist and managing director William T. Wilson in a report).[15]

INDIA: ON THE CUSP OF SOMETHING BIG

One could quibble with the optimists about the extent of the coming transformation in India's economy. There will be a host of very valid questions about the quality and consequences of the growth. How will its gains be distributed? Will decades of high economic growth further strain natural resources like water and oil? Will regional inequality worsen and strain the federal political system? Every country has had to deal with similar issues during its years of high growth. To believe that India will be different is plain myopia. But there is a trade-off here. The alternative to high growth — with all its attendant problems — is low growth and the curse of mass poverty. Economists are the natural party of growth; not because they are blind to its pitfalls, but because the alternative is inevitably worse.

There is today more reason to be optimistic about India's prospects than ever before. Bangalore has become a metaphor of what India is capable of. The city acts as an excellent advertisement for the entire country. But India is more than Bangalore. The Indian economy is more than software firms and call centers. You will see a new spirit of confidence in towns and villages across the subcontinent. It could be the business magnate eyeing a foreign acquisition, the poor taxi driver doing all he can to put his child through school, the young entrepreneur striving for his first sale. Millions of Indians still live on the edge of desperation. They can be pulled into the comfort of prosperity only if the economy keeps growing at its current pace (or faster) for another 20 years.

India is on the cusp of something big. But let's not forget that India spent most of the 20th century in stagnation despite an initial show of promise during the last decades of the 19th century. What went wrong? It will help if we examine why the last century was a tragic period of lost opportunities for the Indian economy. The next chapter is a flashback on an era that trapped millions in poverty and disease.

NOTES

1. Quoted by Mark Steyn in an article in *The Washington Post* on May 9, 2004.
2. Quoted by Cesar Conda and Stuart Anderson in their article "Traders Are Not Traitors" in *The Weekly Standard*, March 29, 2004.
3. Paul Samuelson: "Where Ricardo and Mill Rebut and Confirm Arguments of Mainstream Economists Supporting Globalisation", *Journal of Economic Perspectives*, Summer 2004.
4. N. Gregory Mankiw and Phillip Swagel: "The Politics and Economics of Offshore Outsourcing", *American Enterprise Institute* Working Paper No. 122, December 7, 2005.
5. "The World in the iPod", by Andrew Leonard; *Der Spiegel*, August 8, 2005.
6. "A New World Economy", by Pete Engardio; *BusinessWeek*, August 22, 2005.
7. Raghuram Rajan: "Making India A Global Hub", a speech reprinted in the *McKinsey Quarterly* 2005 Special Edition, Fulfilling India's Promise.
8. "Korea, 1964: Economic Miracle", by Joan Robinson, *Monthly Review*, January 1965.
9. From an interview with Pawar by Shekhar Gupta, *Indian Express*, November 15, 2005.
10. From http://www.nobelprize.org, the official website of the Nobel Prize committee.
11. *The Return of Depression Economics*, by Paul Krugman, *Penguin Books*, 1999.
12. Quoted in "The Long Race", by Niranjan Rajadhyaksha, *Business World*, December 5, 2005.
13. "Dreaming of BRICs: The Path To 2050", by Dominic Wilson and Roopa Purshothaman, *Global Economics Paper No. 99*, Goldman Sachs.
14. "India Rising: A Medium Term Perspective", by Jennifer Asuncion-Mund, *Deutsche Bank Research*, May 19, 2005.
15. "The Dawn of the Indian Century", by William T. Wilson, *Keystone India*.

2

A Century of Lost Opportunities

Assume for a moment that you are living at end of the 19th century. Japan has already had its Meiji Restoration and is rapidly transforming itself into a modern economy. You have been allowed to place a bet on the Asian country that is most likely to follow Japan's footsteps. Which country would you choose? Your most sensible call would be to put your money on the country that has a growing manufacturing sector, a modern network of ports and railways, a new educated class, an efficient bureaucracy, and links to the biggest commercial enterprise of the day — the British Empire at the peak of its power. In other words, you would choose India.

Placing such bets is always a hazardous business, and this one would be yet another in the long list of "sure bets" that eventually did not work out. India was overtaken by country after country in Asia during the 20th century. Why did India lose out? That is one question that always brings forth various answers. The standard nationalist answer is that the colonial government impoverished India and transferred wealth out of the country. Liberal economists would insist that India suffered because successive governments, in both the colonial and independent eras, preferred protectionism to free trade. Then there are the many explanations rooted in the social structure. India's rigid caste system and male-dominated social structure in effect denied access to education and skills to the vast majority; there was no meaningful land reform after Independence to create incomes and demand in the rural areas; and some cultural determinists would argue that India's cultural values are not conducive to hard work and risk-taking.

I would not even try to suggest which theory provides the best explanation for India's economic stagnation during the past 100 years. It is one of those grand questions that will keep academics and the seminar crowd busy for many decades to come. Yet, the incontrovertible fact is that India could have started breaking out of its poverty trap in the second half of the 19th century but failed to do so. Historians often speak of India's unfinished cultural renaissance in the 19th century — a variety of social and religious reforms that challenged the existing order but could never be taken to their logical conclusion. And as a result of this unfinished cultural renaissance, Indian society continued to have a curious combination of modernity and superstition.

Something similar happened in economics. The initial hopes that the economy would deliver a better life to millions of people living in the Indian subcontinent were sadly belied. To capture the optimism and the aspirations of those times, let us trek back to the year 1893 and to an accidental meeting between a monk and a merchant.

AN ACCIDENTAL MEETING

Sometime in that year, a ship called the *Empress of India* sailed from Yokohama in Japan to Vancouver in Canada. On board were two extraordinary Indians — Swami Vivekananda and Jamshetji Tata. Both were headed for Chicago, which was to host the World's Columbian Exposition, a celebration of technology and industrial progress. It was here that an engineer named Gale Ferris put up the first Ferris wheel and where a small businessman named Milton Hershey saw a German machine to make chocolate, and is said to have told a cousin: "Caramel is only a fad. Chocolate is a permanent thing."

Tata was undoubtedly going to Chicago to get new business ideas. This was the era of the robber barons in the United States — people like railroad financier Jay Gould who triggered a stock market crash in 1869 or steel magnate Henry Frick who was shot dead by a business rival. Tata was a businessman of a different sort. He was a world removed from the robber barons and their raw greed. Tata was interested in his country's progress in addition to his own profits. He (like many other merchant princes of the time) had made his initial fortune in the opium trade with China, had started one of the first textile mills in India, and was later to challenge established wisdom with his battle to set up a steel plant in India (it was eventually set up in 1907, three years after his death). He had even experimented with a remarkably modern governance system in one of his companies. Tata was for two years a salaried managing director reporting to an independent board of directors, many decades before all this became fashionable.[1]

Vivekananda was a restless soul and an unusual man of religion. He wanted to free India from the deadening grip of outdated social customs. He once said that religion was of no use to a hungry man. Vivekananda was on his way to Chicago to attend a smaller show that was meant to compliment the industrial exhibition: the World's Parliament of Religions. He was an unknown monk when he stood on the stage to give his speech on September 11, 1893. The French writer Romain Rolland writes in his biography of Vivekananda "... his speech was like a tongue of flame. Among the grey wastes of cold dissertation it fired the souls of the listening throng."[2] Vivekananda returned home a hero, and became an inspiration to generations of Indians.

What we are interested in here is that chance meeting between the monk and the merchant on board the *Empress of India*. Vivekananda was passionate about science and development. Tata was a keen supporter of social reform. It was a meeting of two visionaries. On board the ship, they are said to have discussed Tata's plan to start a steel mill in India. It is believed that the Swami told Tata that there were two parts to the challenge — manufacturing technology and the science of steel. The former could be bought from abroad but the science had to be researched at home. This seeded the idea in Tata's mind to start what was to become the Indian Institute of Science in Bangalore. It was to be the first center for scientific research in the country. The choice of location for the new research institute would prove to be prophetic. Bangalore would eventually become a breeding ground of scientists and engineers, and hence the natural home of India's software companies a hundred years later. Tata later wrote to Vivekananda in 1898, asking for his support for the venture: "I know not who would make a more fitting general of such a campaign than Vivekananda."[3]

GLOBALIZATION VER 1.0

The year Tata wrote his letter was to mark the end of a period of modest — but volatile — growth in the Indian economy. There were no official statistics then, but many economists have worked backwards to estimate the size of the Indian economy in those years. National income, according to one estimate, grew at an average annual rate of 1.1% between the years 1860 and 1900. Since population growth was as low as 0.4% a year in these 40 years, average incomes grew at 0.7%. These were very modest growth rates, but significant nevertheless, because they marked a clear break from many centuries of economic stagnation. Incomes were growing after a long period of stagnation.

This was India in the midst of the first wave of globalization. New technologies, falling transport costs, and free capital flows were stringing together economies around the world. India too was breaking out of its old economic structure. The Great Indian Peninsula Railway was built in 1863 to connect Bombay to the cotton-growing districts of the interior. The first telegraph line between India and Europe was laid in 1866. The Suez Canal was opened to traffic three years later. It was a time of tentative optimism, and one case of crazed euphoria.

A few years before the train, the ship, and the telegraph tied many parts of India to the world economy, the country's financial capital experienced an episode of madness and panic that was to have a deep impact on subsequent economic developments. The US Civil War broke out in 1861. Till then, the textile mills in England sourced only about 20% of their cotton from India. When the Confederacy ports in the cotton-growing south were blockaded, exports from the United States to England came to a halt. The demand for Indian cotton shot through the roof, and so did prices. The abnormal profits that were earned from the cotton trade were recycled into banks, shipping companies, and land development schemes. One thing led to another, and soon Bombay (as Mumbai was then known) was in the grip of a full-fledged speculative frenzy. The schemes got more and more crazy. A bubble was blown.

BOOM AND BUST: AN EPISODE OF SPECULATIVE FRENZY

The greatest speculator of this age was Premchand Roychand. He made a fortune as a crafty cotton trader. Roychand operated before the telegraph line between India and Europe was laid, before information about prices could be transmitted with ease across continents. Roychand had a neat trick up his sleeve.

He would send his agents out on country boats to meet the ships coming in from England. Their task was to get the latest London prices before the ships docked in Bombay. Local prices aligned themselves with global prices only after the ships were docked and the sailors came on land to give the news from London. Roychand's advance guard of data collectors gave him a head start over other cotton traders in Bombay. Armed with his privileged information, Roychand would take his positions in the cotton market even before the others knew what was happening.[4] As with all financial bubbles, this one too, popped. Prices crashed in 1865, as the Civil War came to an end in the United States. Cotton prices came back to more sensible levels. Bombay was a graveyard of lost fortunes. Roychand too was wiped out and had to start life afresh. Many of those who burnt their fingers in the crash swore off all risk-taking. The first cotton mills built by Indian businessmen had come up in the 1850s. But no new cotton mill came up in Bombay between 1860 and 1872, first because of the obsessive financial speculation and then because of the crash.

The swing between extreme gambling and extreme caution killed honest enterprise. Twelve new mills were built between July 1873 and December 1874 and another 20 over the next four years. India's textile industry was humming again.[5] Soon, the cotton magnates of Manchester were crying foul. The colonial government tried to help the Manchester men by abolishing the 7.5% import duty on some textile goods in 1875, though a minor tariff on textile imports in general was maintained.

"This cotton boom has already been noticed as marking the advent of a new economic era in India. Its aftermath was also typical of the new conditions that were being introduced. The trade crisis, which followed the reckless floating of companies for all possible and impossible purposes and the resulting collapse of all credit, was the first of its kind in India. The collapse of credit in Bombay in 1865 was indeed so complete that normal conditions were not restored till 1871.... The crisis, however, had one good result for the cotton mill industry. It demonstrated the impracticability of the numerous schemes that had been launched during the boom period and also showed that the cotton industry was the only stable and profitable industry" (the economist D.R. Gadgil in his classic *The Industrial Evolution of India*).[6]

THE DAWN OF INDIAN INDUSTRY

Most of India's early industrial base — dominated by textile mills — was built with domestic capital and enterprise. The business history of these times is full of stories of men who struggled against immense odds to set up modern business enterprises.

Many ventured out abroad. A newsletter of the Royal Asiatic Society of Hong Kong says: "In the first 25 years of Hong Kong's history, as many as a quarter of all foreign firms in Hong Kong belonged to Parsee Zoroastrians." These *taipans* (like Sir Jamshetjee Jeejeeboy, a Parsee, and David Sassoon, a Jew from Baghdad who made Bombay his base for some time) brought the first banking and insurance businesses to the city and were founding members of the Hong Kong and Shanghai Bank (known today as the Hong Kong and Shanghai Banking Corporation) in 1865.[7] The setting up of the bank itself was a response to the news

> "that a group of financiers in Bombay were forming their own Bank of China, to be chartered in London and based in Hong Kong, but with no more than a small fraction of its shares allocated to the China-coast business community it was intended to serve" (www.chamber.org.hk, the website of the Hong Kong General Chamber of Commerce).[7]

The point of this short trip through India's early business history is to try and show that it is erroneous to argue that Indian culture is incapable of fostering enterprise. In fact, many centuries earlier, this is what the French traveler Tavernier had to say about the traders he met in the western parts of India: "The Jews engaged in money matters in the Turkish Empire are usually considered to be exceptionally able, but they are scarcely fit to be apprenticed to the money changers of India."[8]

While it was domestic capital that built local manufacturing, foreign capital had a significant role in funding the development of infrastructure. The British government was building a network of roads and railways, originally meant to move troops around the country but later to get cotton and other commodities for export to England. This infrastructure — which preceded economic growth rather than the other way round as is the case today — was financed through bonds raised in the London market at highly competitive rates. Government guarantees helped India boast one of the lowest costs of capital in the world between 1870 and 1913.

THE DRAIN THEORY

These were the years when India consistently had budgetary surpluses. The colonial government used these surpluses to take capital out of the country. Early nationalist leaders like Dadabhai Naoroji hit out at this drain. Some of this drain was because of interest payments to foreign creditors and hence not too much of an issue to the modern eye. The most contentious of the various outflows from colonial India were the so-called home charges, or the expenses incurred in England to run the Empire in India. This included everything from the cost of running the British army in India to the salaries and pensions paid to the top imperial officials. In effect, Indians were paying their foreign rulers — to be kept in servitude (modern economists could perhaps blandly define home charges as invisibles). These home charges accounted for around a quarter of the Indian government's total budget, and effectively ensured that money was not available for more pressing local needs, from domestic investment to famine relief.

Despite the drain, India at the end of the 19th century was an economy that was stirring after centuries of torpor. It was in many ways an open economy with export-led growth. P.R. Brahmanada, one of the country's most respected economists after Independence, in his monumental *Money, Income, and Prices in 19th Century India*, estimates that industrial production grew at an astonishing 8.4% a year between 1861 and 1900.[9] India was an early beneficiary of the first wave of globalization, whereas now it is a late beneficiary of the second.

India's share of world trade at the end of the 19th century was 7% (currently, after many decades of destructive protectionism, it is around 1.5%). There was a trade surplus during most of this period. By 1913, India had attracted $2.1 billion ($7 per capita) of foreign capital. China had only $1.6 billion ($3.6 per capita). Agricultural production too increased a bit, because new land was brought under cultivation and the area under irrigation increased. Meghnad Desai, economist and a peer in the House of Lords, argues too that the drain did not do as much harm as the early nationalists believed. Assuming that 2% of India's national income was drained out every year to England, Desai estimates that India lost about 0.15% of GDP growth a year.[10]

Would this extra 0.15% a year have been enough to lift millions out of poverty? Perhaps not; but when the economy was growing at just above 1% a year, the drain kept growth rates about 10% lower than they would otherwise have been. Compound that over half a century, and you would see that while the drain was not as important as the early nationalist critics assumed, it was not some trifle either.

THE FEAR OF FOREIGN TRADE

The Indian economy, and especially its industrial sector, was driven by domestic enterprise and foreign trade during the 19th century. This did not last for too long. Country after country turned its back on foreign trade soon after, and protectionism reached its zenith in the years between the two World Wars. India's economy stalled, partly as a result of the fact that foreign trade was mistakenly equated with political servitude.

India turned its back on the global economy for nearly a century. And paid the price for it. Some of the most enlightened nationalist leaders of this era clamored for higher tariffs to protect India's young industries. To many of them, foreign trade was not something to be abhorred nor was it something to be blindly sought.

> "They favoured import of machines and raw material and export of manufactured goods. They even espoused the cause of increasing imports of manufactured goods, provided India was economically prospering, and not declining, and provided such imports promoted, and not retarded, economic growth" (historian Bipan Chandra in his *The Rise and Growth of Economic Nationalism In India*).[11]

The early nationalists had a far more progressive view on foreign trade than the men and women who designed the first economic policies in independent India. Yet, their support to exports and imports was a bit too tentative. Meanwhile, the colonial government did its dirigiste bit too. The liberal economist Deepak Lal writes:

> "...the British departed from the twin policies of free trade and *laissez faire* ... which had led India to be a pioneer of Third World industrialisation, based on domestic capital and

entrepreneurship and imported technology. The breakdown of
the global economy for the half-century from the first world war
further eroded the incipient integration of India in the world
economy, which had occurred during the British Raj."[12]

It was many decades before the lessons of the 19th century were
learnt.

THE DOORS ARE SHUT

If there is an economist's version of the original sin, it is
protectionism. Trade helps countries specialise, fosters competition
and is a vehicle for the transfer of technology and knowledge.
India sinned in spectacular fashion through the first four decades
after independence in 1947. It shut itself from the world economy,
and paid a heavy price.

The most severe attacks on independent India's early economic
strategy target national planning and the obsession with heavy
industry. I think the fear of global trade was an equally important
drawback, if not the most important. By 1990, India had one of
the highest rates of protection in the world. The Asian
Development Bank showed in 1997 that the open economies of
Asia grew 2% faster than the closed economies in the continent
between 1965 and 1990. In the latter year, just before it belatedly
embraced liberal economic policies, India had one of the world's
highest rates of protection.

It is now fashionable to lay every subsequent ill at the door of
Jawaharlal Nehru, the first prime minister of independent India.
Nehru's vision of a modern and industrial India cannot be faulted.
The way he went about it was deeply flawed, however. Nehru was
a product of his times. India was a keen follower of the economic
consensus of the 1950s, which held that national planning and
protectionism were the way forward. To varying degrees, the
suspicion of private enterprise, free markets, and foreign trade was
endemic in the political class. One significant exception to this rule
was the brilliant and erudite C. Rajagopalachari, one of Mahatma
Gandhi's political heirs who set up the liberal Swatantra Party to
fight against what he memorably called the license-permit raj.
Meanwhile, even India's business class was a votary of national
planning and protectionism.

"PRICELESS" PLANNING AND OTHER ABSURDITIES

Many of the world's renowned economists were invited to India in the 1950s to advise the government on policy, so the quality of advice was top class. Yet, these economists indirectly gave India a maddening web of controls that all but killed the desire to work and invest. Peter Bauer, then a lone voice fighting the conventional wisdom in development economics, once wrote about a meeting he had with a senior civil servant from the Gold Coast (today's Ghana) in the early 1960s. This bureaucrat told Bauer: "… economics was irrelevant to Africa because the African simply did not respond to economic motives."[13]

India did not go that far down the road to economic illiteracy, but those neat and impressive planning models of the 1950s never delivered growth. Bauer criticized sophisticated economic models "in which the abstraction and aggregation involved render them irrelevant … they become travesties which divert attention from the essentials and obscure the issues."[14] Indian economic planning had plenty of abstraction and aggregation. Looking back, it now seems strange that economic policy and plans were so completely divorced from that basic unit of economic data — price. The government planned for output, without paying too much attention to prices. India's five-year plans were priceless — that is, "price-less" — though in the wrong sort of way.

MILTON FRIEDMAN IN INDIA

Among the economists who came to India was Milton Friedman. He was an unusual visitor, in the sense that he was deeply skeptical of what India was trying to do at a time when most of his peers were admirers of planning and protectionism. Friedman once wrote about his experiences in India. He tells an interesting story of how well-intentioned policies to protect domestic companies can often have perverse results. Friedman had owned a 1950 Buick car that he sold in the United States before he came over to India. He got $50 for the car. He was surprised to find that the same model was selling at a steep $1,500–2,000 at the official exchange rate and over $1,000 at the market exchange rate. Trade would have equalized prices for a second-hand Buick in India and the United States. That was not to be. Car prices were just one example of the sort of damage import controls had wrought. "Clearly the sensible and cheap way for India to get automobile transportation is to import second-hand cars and trucks from abroad," Friedman wrote. That would have been sacrilege — wasting precious foreign exchange on cars when we can make them ourselves! India, in effect, noted Friedman, was saying that "we are too poor to buy secondhand motor cars, (so) we must buy new ones."[15]

The same story repeated itself in all sorts of industrial goods. India was trapped in an inefficient and high-cost economy. A few economists did argue for a more export-friendly strategy. One of them was Manmohan Singh, later to become the country's reformist finance minister and then prime minister. His doctoral thesis at Oxford, in 1964, was an attempt to show why India should export more so as to earn foreign exchange and cut its dependence on foreign aid. A few years later, in 1969, Jagdish Bhagwati and Padma Desai launched a broader attack on India's economic policies. Bhagwati, who would later emerge as one of the most influential voices on the side of free trade but then a mainstream Indian economist, was a convert. He recalls a visit to Japan at the end of the 1950s in an interview to V.N. Balasubramanyam. "I was talking to Saburo Okita, the Japanese economist, and telling him — 'you don't understand that external markets are tight, you can't promote exports and therefore import-substitution was desirable for Japan too'." And this advice was given when Japan was on the cusp of the great export-led economic boom that would transform its economic fortunes.[16]

A FEW EARLY DISSENTERS FROM BOMBAY

Curiously, the worst protectionism came quite by accident, but then lingered on for too long. In 1957, India had its first major balance of payments crisis. The showpiece second five-year plan had come into effect the year before. It borrowed heavily from the Soviet experience. Two Bombay economists — C.N. Vakil and P.R. Brahmananda — had already criticized the obsession with heavy industry and the neglect of consumer goods and agriculture (or what they called wage goods).

The central feature of the second plan was an ambitious investment program to build new plants in industries such as steel and fertilizers. Domestic savings were not enough to fund the new industrial ventures, so the plan depended on foreign funding. Few seemed to detect the flaws in the plan at that time, though they seem quite obvious now. The lone exception was B.R. Shenoy, who was once described as the only liberal economist between Athens and Tokyo. In his neglected dissent note to the approach paper to the second plan, Shenoy had warned about a looming balance of payments crisis and a spike in inflation because of the plan's ambitious investment targets. But he, like his teacher at the London School of Economics, Friedrich von Hayek, was a prophet in the wilderness.

WHY FOREIGN INVESTMENT WENT ELSEWHERE: AN EXAMPLE

The balance of payments crisis that Shenoy had predicted sent the government into a tizzy. These were the years of "export pessimism" — the belief that a poor country could not depend on foreign markets as a source of growth. The way out of a balance of payments problem, it was believed, was to crack down on imports. A frightening edifice of import controls came up. There were other insanities. Foreign investment was looked upon with suspicion. Here is one example, a story of another Tata recounted in the book *Business Legends* by business historian Gita Piramal. In 1954, J.R.D. Tata was on a plane to Geneva. With him were his legal advisor J.D. Choksi and Sumant Moolgaokar of Tata Engineering and Locomotive Company (Telco). The company was doing only one thing — selling locomotives to the Indian Railways. Tata, who headed the conglomerate that grew out of Jamshetji's early ventures, wanted to break this dependence on just one customer. He had read that the German auto giant Daimler Benz was trying to find a partner in Asia. The meeting was to be held in Geneva. The two sides agreed to become partners in a venture to make trucks in India.[17]

It was tough going. Suffocating controls on private-sector investment were tightened further. The Tariff Commission of 1953 had come to the mind-boggling conclusion that only those automobile companies that already had a manufacturing program would be allowed to make cars and trucks. In effect, new players were banned from entering the business. The market was to be left to five companies — Hindustan Motors, Premier Automobiles, Standard Motor Products, Automobile Products of India, and Ashok Motors. Imports, needless to say, were discouraged. This was an open invitation to poor quality and high costs.

Thankfully, Tata managed to convince the government to waive these ridiculous restrictions, and Telco started manufacturing trucks. The success of the venture sparked off a desire to manufacture cars as well. "We feel the time has come to move into the small car field where there is likely ultimately to be an unlimited market," Tata wrote in a letter to his friend George Woods, who was the president of the World Bank at that time.

> "In 1960, Telco loaned four Mercedes-Benz cars to K.B. Lal, secretary of commerce and industry in the Indian government, to use for a year before taking a decision. Another car went to V.K. Krishna Menon, the defence minister. The cars were much appreciated, but no decision was taken and they were returned. The Germans hung around for a while but eventually decided they couldn't wait any longer and located their Mercedes assembly plant in Singapore instead of India" (Piramal).[17]

It was only 30 years later than Mercedes-Benz came back to India to make cars in collaboration with Telco.

A POLICY MESS

Domestic investment was shackled, foreign trade shriveled and foreign capital was kept out. India turned its back not just on money, but also on the efficiency and knowledge that come with trade and investment. The domestic economy too was bound in a complex and bewildering web of controls. Entire industries were reserved for the public sector and the small-scale sector. Companies could not make things without a license from the government. Despite rampant shortages, it was a crime to produce more than what you were allowed. Agriculture was neglected. Consumers were forced to buy all sorts of shoddy and expensive goods. The few companies that had government licenses (often because they had paid a bribe to the bureaucrats who gave these licenses) could make huge profits in the absence of any meaningful competition.

All this is not to say that there were no bright spots. India continued to diversify its industrial base. Though primary education was neglected, investments in institutes of higher learning (especially technical colleges) laid the base for subsequent successes in skill-based manufacturing and software services. Economic management was prudent, thus ensuring that inflation never went to Latin American levels. Debt and deficits were modest.

But the bad economics never went away. The way India chose between capital and labor is just one of the most shocking examples of bad policy. One does not need learned treatises on technology choices to know that something was terribly wrong. India was an economy that was short on capital and rich in labor. The natural course of action would have been to promote labor-intensive manufacturing. India had already had a head start in some industries like textiles that could employ people in large numbers. Yet, the government continued to be obsessed with heavy industries like steel. Interest rates were kept artificially low, often below the inflation rate. So companies could borrow at zero cost in a capital-scarce economy. Here was an incentive to use more capital than labor, and fritter it away. Meanwhile, the small-scale sector was a protected niche where labor was used inefficiently. Hundreds of goods were reserved exclusively for small units, regardless of their efficiency.

In retrospect, this web of regulation looks like a web of insanity. And the funny thing is that it was designed by some of the world's best economists. Perhaps there is some truth in the cynical quip that India's problem is that it had too many good economists!

THE GREAT CONVERGENCE

One *stylized* view of economic history of the world neatly divides it into three eras. The first era covers most of recorded human history. Societies battled against nature and barely produced enough to feed the population. Population often outstripped food supply and people starved to death. Incomes were stagnant. Poverty was endemic. Then some countries started moving ahead after the Industrial Revolution in Europe. This was the second era in economic history. Global incomes diverged. The world got divided into rich countries and poor countries. The third stage started somewhere at the turn of the 19th century. The gap between incomes in some of the erstwhile poor countries and those in the rich countries started narrowing. Economies started converging, though at different points of time and at different speeds.

In 1988, economists William Baumol and Edward Wolff explained the process of economic development in terms of membership of a convergence club.[18] The productivity levels in some countries started moving towards those in the rich countries, thanks to technology transfer, the spread of education and a rise in international trade and investment. There is still a substantial debate whether differences in productivity and incomes have increased or decreased over the past hundred years or so. But many countries — from Japan to Chile — have converged towards the West in the past century. (There are also the rare cases of countries that started converging and then reversed course. Most of the examples are to be found in Latin America and the countries that were part of the former Soviet Union. Some countries in Western Africa — like Ghana — did show promise in the 1940s as the war demand for commodities like rubber sparked off fast growth here.)

Angus Maddison's astonishing study of incomes through history tells a neat tale. His data shows the pattern on India's divergence and convergence very clearly. In 1700, India was one of the world's stronger economies. It is no accident that European adventurers set sail to trade with it. India's textiles and spices were sought after in cities like London, Paris, and Lisbon. Maddison estimates that the per capita income in Britain was about 11 times that in India in 1700. For what was to become the United States, the multiple was a little less than five times. By 1820, the average Briton was about 16 times richer than the average Indian and the average US citizen was about 12 times richer. In 1950, a little after India became independent, the differentials had climbed to 55 times (Britain) and 77 times (United States). By 1980, it was 68 and 100 times, respectively. What started as a relatively modest gap in 1700 became a wide chasm more than 280 years later.[19] Then, at last, the gap started narrowing. By 2000, incomes in Britain were 51 times greater than incomes in India. For the United States, it was 74 times. The gap between India and these countries is still huge, but the trend is towards a narrowing. Avinash Celestine, my colleague at *Business World*, once drew a nifty graph that married Madisson's data with the long-term forecasts of Goldman Sachs. It shows with great clarity the process of divergence and convergence for India. I have reproduced the graph on page 44.

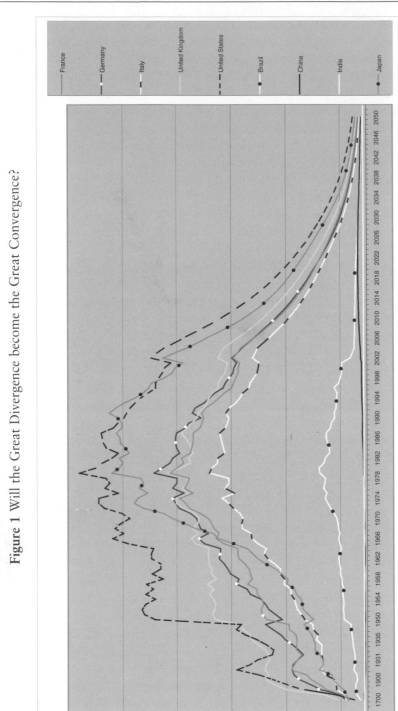

Figure 1 Will the Great Divergence become the Great Convergence?

THE EARLY REFORMS

The turning point is 1980. Before we start looking at why Indian incomes started converging towards those in countries like Britain and the United States after 1980, let us examine why they diverged in the first place. India accounted for 25% of the world's industrial output in 1700. That had dropped precipitously to 2% by 1900. Why? There were many factors at play. Colonial exploitation was obviously one of them. It meant everything from unfavorable terms of trade to outright looting. But that is not the whole story. Modern research shows there were two other significant shocks to Indian industry — one from the demand side and one from the supply side. The demand-side shock came as a result of the Industrial Revolution in Britain Improvements in technology raised the productivity levels of British textile workers. Transport costs too fell at the same time. As a result, global textile prices dropped. Indian textile manufacturers could not compete as British rivals captured their markets — first abroad and then at home. The supply side shock came from high food prices that pushed up real wages in India. The dissolution of the Mughal Empire and India's slow decline into internal wars and anarchy hit farm productivity. Successive droughts made it worse. Food became expensive. Once again, Indian textile manufacturers were hit.

The convergence started in 1980. That year, India saw a change of national government. Indira Gandhi, who had been voted out of office in 1977 because of her brief flirtation with authoritarianism, came back to power. Her new government turned its back on the old socialist legacy, suspicion of private capital, and fear of the foreigner. The first tentative reforms were initiated. India went in for an IMF loan in 1981, after it was sent reeling by a drought and the second oil shock of 1979. The IMF too goaded the government to change its ways. Indira Gandhi's son Rajiv tried to push reforms further after he became prime minister in 1984. The worst of the industrial licensing was done away with, the vice-like grip on imports was loosened, some tax rates were reduced a bit and the rupee was allowed to drift down in a bid to help exports.

The reforms paid off in terms of higher economic growth. It averaged 5.81% in the 1980s, far higher than the 2.95% in the 1970s. This initial liberalization was deeply flawed, however. What the government did was merely to ease some of the restrictions on the growth of domestic companies. It was a godsend for established companies in India, since they had greater operational freedom without the discipline of global competition. Profit margins soared. Consumers benefited less than producers. At the same time, the governments in the 1980s turned their backs on fiscal prudence. Public debt and deficits exploded. India was on the road to bankruptcy.

In 1990–1991, for a few anxious months, India was on the verge of a Latin American style balance of payments crisis. The trade deficit ballooned as oil prices went up after Saddam Hussain's invasion of Kuwait. Capital fled the country. At one point of time, there was barely enough money with the Reserve Bank of India (RBI) to pay for 15 days of essential imports. The nation's gold was mortgaged to raise emergency funds. The IMF was eventually approached.

THE NEW DELHI CONSENSUS

The new government that came to power under the leadership of Narasimha Rao in July 1991 started off with an inspired move. It asked Manmohan Singh, one of the country's top economists and administrators, to become finance minister. Like many insiders who had realized that the old path was leading India nowhere, Manmohan Singh had already been converted to the virtues of an open economy. He dismantled the worst parts of the old system in a few swift strokes.

Since then, economic reforms have had their ups and downs. But the general direction of policy has been towards greater economic freedom. The reformists have often been accused of being servants of global capital and unthinking admirers of the so-called Washington Consensus, the world-view held by the triad of the IMF, World Bank, and the US Treasury. Nothing could be further from the truth. In fact, India has differed with the Washington Consensus on various counts. Economic policy has been far more nuanced than the supporters of statism realize. The Indian government has not sold its assets aggressively in privatization programs. The opening up of the tradables sector has been faster than that of non-tradables (like banking and retailing). Capital account convertibility has been handled very carefully, step by step. And there has been no fiscal fundamentalism; the government has not attacked its budget deficit with the single-minded determination that the Washington trio normally encourages. So there are significant ways in which India has stuck to its own "middle path," as Narasimha Rao described it in an important speech at Davos in early 1994. We could also call this the "New Delhi consensus."

Economic policy in India after Independence went through three stages before 1990. The first was the optimism of the 1950s that a planned economy and rapid industrialization would allow India to emerge out of centuries of economic darkness. Then there was the despair of the 1970s that things were not working out, but still there was no honest acceptance of what the problem really was. People tried to tinker at the peripheries of the system right through the 1980s. Finally, there was an honest appraisal of what had gone wrong and successive rounds of radical reforms in the 1990s. India is back to where it was in the 1950s — there is a new sense of confidence about the future. The wheel has come full circle.

NOTES

1. *The Oxford History of Indian Business*, by Dwijendra Tripathi, Oxford University Press, 2004.
2. *Vivekananda*, by Romain Rolland, Advaita Ashram, Calcutta, 1988, p.37.
3. From http://www.tata.com, the website of the Tata Group.
4. *City Of Gold: A Biography Of Bombay*, by Gillian Tendall, Penguin, 1982, p.176.
5. This information is culled from *The Oxford History of Indian Business*, by Dwijendra Tripathi; Oxford University Press, 2004.
6. *The Industrial Evolution of India*, by D.R. Gadgil, Oxford University Press, 1924, pp.52–53.
7. Royal Asiatic Society Hong Kong Branch; http://www.royalasiaticsociety.org. hk/newsletters/2003_12.pdf.
8. *The Oxford History Of Indian Business*, by Dwijendra Tripathi, Oxford University Press, 2004, p.21.
9. *Money, Income, Prices in 19th Century India*, by P.R. Brahmananda, Himalaya Publishing House, 2001.
10. "Drains, Hoards and Foreigners: Does The Nineteenth Century Indian Economy Have Any Lessons For The Twenty First Century India", by Meghnad Desai, First P.R. Brahmanand Memorial Lecture, available at: http://rbidocs.rbi.org.in/ rdocs/Speeches/DOCs/57121.doc.
11. *The Rise and Growth of Economic Nationalism in India*, by Bipan Chandra, New Delhi: People's Publishing House, 1966.
12. Available at: http://www.econ.ucla.edu/lal; the home page of Deepak Lal.
13. *Economic Analysis and Policy in Underdeveloped Countries*, by P.T. Bauer, Greenwood Press, Reprint 1981, pp.15–16.

14. Quoted by Israel M. Kirzner in his article on "Bauer, Human Attitudes and Economic Growth", *Cato Journal*, Vol. 25, No. 3, Fall 2005.
15. These anecdotes and quotes are from *Friedman on India*, edited by Parth J. Shah, New Delhi: Centre For Civil Society, 2000.
16. *Conversations with Indian Economists*, by V.N. Balasubramanyam, Macmillan India, 2001, p.145.
17. This anecdote is from *Business Legends*, by Gita Piramal, Viking, 1998, pp.487–488.
18. A brief article by J. Bradford Long on the convergence club is available at: http://www.j-bradford-delong.net/Econ_Articles/Dowrick/conv_club.html.
19. http://www.ggdc.net/Maddison/; the home page of Angus Maddison.

Chapter 3

People Power

THE POWER OF A BILLION AND MORE

A little girl was born at the Safdarjang Hospital in New Delhi in the early hours of May 11, 2000. Her birth was announced amidst an impatient throng of reporters and cameramen. A few politicians too landed there to see the baby. Hospital guards reportedly climbed on the bed where mother and child lay, and used wooden clubs to beat back the crowd. "Do not crush the baby!" a minister screamed into her microphone. The baby's early moments of fame were not because she was a child of rich, famous, or glamorous parents. The father worked in a car parts shop and earned a modest Rs. 2,200 ($50) a month while the mother managed their house. They were definitely not one of the beautiful people around whom the Indian media flits in breathless excitement.

The girl was named Aastha, or "faith" in Hindi. Aastha was one of the approximately 42,000 children who were born in India on the day when India's population crossed a billion. It thus became only the second country after China to have a billion or more citizens. Actually, any one of the 42,000 kids born that day could have been the billionth Indian. There was no way of knowing for sure. But the government's spin-doctors had to choose one child to symbolically celebrate the event. They chose Aastha, and the press and politicians were there to take advantage of the moment, though in their differing ways.

It was not all bouquets and flashbulbs, however. The Prime Minister, Atal Bihari Vajpayee, said he was worried that the population had crossed a billion, and that this was "a serious matter that is the cause for both concern and introspection."

He also announced a new policy that would aim to stabilize the country's population by 2045 and set up a 100-member commission to advise him how to go about the task (Indian politicians and bureaucrats can put Sir Humphrey Appleby, the devious mandarin in the hit BBC TV comedy series *Yes Minister* and *Yes Prime Minister* to shame with their enthusiasm for setting up committees, commissions, working groups, and task forces). Meanwhile, at the Safdarjang Hospital, the baby was passed around from politician to smiling politician, was made to suffer the heat of the arc lights that the photographers had flashed on her delicate face, was the subject of inane speeches — and was then quickly forgotten.

SO MANY PEOPLE: BLESSING OR CURSE?

There has been no news of little Aastha since then. The chances are that she will have to struggle to overcome many obstacles. After all, she was born in a country where one out of every ten babies does not live to see its fifth birthday; where girls do not get the sort of pampered treatment reserved for their brothers; where 40 million children do not attend school; where malnutrition of children is common. Childhood is often a harsh experience in India. Has Aastha been spared these travails?

There were now well over a billion Indians, and many more millions to come. It is hardly surprising that Aastha's birth was accompanied by a paroxysm of doubt and fear. After all, India already has 17% of the world's population crowded into just 2.2% of the world's land area. There are 29 Indians being born every minute, and over 15 million every year. How will this tide of babies be fed, schooled, and employed? The darkest neo-Malthusian fears once again came to the fore. Few seemed to care that Indians are far better off today than they were a few decades ago, despite a population explosion. India too has benefited from the great wave of productivity that has helped mankind to squeeze more out of the limited resources available on earth. The main obstacle in the path to prosperity in countries like India has not been population growth, but economic and social policies that have put a lid on the creative energies of the average Indian.

Two old questions resurfaced in public debate after Aastha's birth — one macro and one micro. Would the birth of millions of babies over the next few decades crush all hopes of economic prosperity? What sort of life would Aastha and others like her hope to live in 21st century India? The two questions were very closely related to each other. Individual welfare and economic growth are inextricably linked. The manner in which the children being born in India will live depends on how well or poorly the economy does in the future. And future economic performance will in turn depend on whether young Indians have access to food, health care, and education, among other things, so that they can live productive lives. The issue to sort out is whether India (both the government and the citizens) should wait patiently for economic growth to throw up the resources needed to finance wide-ranging educational and health programs or whether money should be diverted from the existing pool of funds for immediate use in schools and hospitals.

India has often been dismissed as a Malthusian basket case, an overpopulated country that is doomed to live in hunger and poverty. That sort of overwhelming pessimism is now history, but the fear of unchecked population growth persists. If you were to stumble into a typical middle-class discussion on the problems facing India, it is very likely that the house will agree that the main problem is overpopulation. It is a sweeping generalization that is rarely questioned. It also acts as a comforting balm for the elite, which is then free to put the blame of poverty at the door of the poor. Their fecundity is the problem. But if population density alone were the problem, Japan would be condemned to poverty while some of the countries in sub-Saharan Africa would be rich beyond their wildest dreams.

THE ROAD TO A BILLION

It is now close to six decades since India became independent and India's population has trebled in these decades. The first census after independence was done in 1951. There were 361 million Indians then. The latest census in 2001 counted 1.02 billion Indians. Most demographers predict that India will be the most populous country in the world within the next two decades. China has managed to put a brake on its population growth because of its economic growth and its repressive one-child policy. India's rate of population growth too is slowing down, but at its own gradual pace. It will be many more decades before the population finally stabilizes. There are likely to be around 1.4 billion Indians by 2025 and 1.6 billion by 2050.

Around 500 million more people in the country will undoubtedly put pressure on various fronts — land, energy, water, and infrastructure. Urbanization will drive hundreds of millions of people into cities that are already choking. The thought of another 500 million around is enough to send the average Indian packed into an overcrowded train or standing in a mile-long queue into a cold sweat. It is no wonder that many continue to be obsessed with the overpopulation bogey.

Yet, there is increasing recognition that India's young and growing population can also be a great asset, especially in an aging world.

DEMOGRAPHY IS DESTINY

I once met a banker who was coming back to India after spending more than a decade in Europe. He was then in his mid-30s. This banker told me something that was both amusing and interesting. He said that he felt like a young man in Europe but became aware of his true age when he came to India. It had nothing to do with the energy-sapping weather in his home country. There was another reason why age caught up with him in India, he said. A man in his mid-30s sitting in a café in Paris or Berlin is likely to be surrounded by people who are older than him. He would be considered part of the younger crowd. In Mumbai or Bangalore, this same fellow will almost certainly find himself in the midst of excitable kids in their teens or twenties who will shoot occasional glances of pity at one so old.

There is more to this story than a casual observation about the clientele in a coffee shop. Changing demographics are now widely recognized as one of the mega-trends of our times, affecting economy, society, and politics. Way back in the 19th century, the French philosopher and sociologist Auguste Comte said presciently that demography is destiny. It is a neat aphorism that is becoming increasingly relevant in the 21st century. Europe (and much of the rich world) is aging while India stays young. There are challenges at both ends of the demographic spectrum — aging societies are struggling to keep their pension systems solvent and young societies have to focus incessantly on education. Yet, the woes of aging societies are likely to provide unexpected advantages for young societies. The gray-haired people on the streets of Europe provide an opportunity for the restless and ambitious young workers in countries like India.

India is headed for a demographic sweet spot that will last for 15 years or so. India's population pyramid will develop a healthy bulge in its middle, a sort of beer belly that, unlike the real thing, is pretty to look at. This bulge in the middle will reflect a happy demographic fact. Demographers divide a population in two groups. Those between the ages of 15 and 60 are in the working age. Those above 60 years of age or below 15 years of age are called dependents. The lower the proportion of dependents, the higher is an economy's ability to invest and grow. India's working-age population is likely to peak over the next decade or so, before it too ages.

India will be one of the few major economies in the world to boast of a youthful population over the next two decades or so. Then it too will catch the global aging virus. The median age of an Indian will start going up. Economic growth tends to rise and then fall in tandem with the broader demographic trend; it has done so in many countries (Table 3).

Table 3
India's Population Pyramid

Age	2000	2025	2050
0–4	11.5	8.2	6.6
5–9	11.1	8.2	6.7
10–14	10.9	8.2	6.7
15–19	10.2	8.1	6.7
20–24	9.2	8.1	6.8
25–29	8.3	8.1	6.8
30–34	7.5	7.9	6.8
35–39	6.6	7.7	6.8
40–44	5.7	7.1	6.7
45–49	4.8	6.3	6.6
50–54	3.9	5.6	6.5
55–59	3.1	4.8	6.1
60–64	2.4	4.0	5.7
65–69	1.8	3.1	4.8
70–74	1.4	2.2	3.8
75–79	0.9	1.4	2.8
80+	0.6	1.2	3.1
Median age of an Indian	23.4	30.8	37.2

Source: US Census Bureau, International Database.

POPULATION AND LABOR

The biggest driver of this immense demographic change is the fertility trend. The average Indian mother is having fewer babies than before. The Total Fertility Rate (TFR) — which is a measure of the number of children per woman — has dropped from 6.5 in 1971 to three in 2003.[1] Demographers say the population of a country stabilizes when the TFR comes down to 2.1 babies per woman. At least nine Indian states and union territories are already close to this replacement level. But another 11 have fertility rates above three, and the list of laggards includes some of the most populous states in north India which hold up the national averages. They are the final frontier of India's pleasant demographic transition.

It is now common, especially in urban India, to come across families with one or two children. There are rational reasons for the change in childbearing habits. Parents would rather put their children through school than send them to work on the farm or in the shop, as they once did. So children, to put it in the heartless language of economics, are becoming cost centers rather than profit centers. That acts as a clear incentive to have fewer of them. The pace at which fertility levels drop further will depend on many other factors — income levels, child mortality rates, contraceptive use, education levels, and the empowerment of the Indian woman. Progress on many of these fronts has been excruciatingly slow, despite impressive economic growth, and democratic politics. One can argue endlessly about the pace of change. What is important, however, is that the overall fertility trend is resolutely downwards.

Fewer children and smaller families have the potential to completely alter the economic prospects of both family and country. How? The fall in fertility levels will drastically bring down the number of dependents per hundred workers, from 45 to 37 according to some estimates. Every man and woman in the working-age group (between 15 and 60) will have fewer dependents to support. The drop in India's dependency ratio could alter its economic destiny. Economists Dani Rodrik of Harvard University and Arvind Subramanian of the International Monetary Fund (IMF) estimate that a 14% fall in the dependency ratio will push up India's savings rate from 25% of GDP to 39%.[2] It is not hard to figure out why. A family with fewer dependants and more working members is likely to save more of its income than before. It works the same way for a country as a whole.

Indians have already started squirreling away a larger portion of their rising incomes. The savings rate, which was around 24% for most of the 1990s, has started inching up. In 2004–2005, it was at an all-time high of 29% and it is likely to keep increasing over the next decade. (There are likely to be factors other than demographics that are pushing up the savings rate, especially higher income levels. It is too early for precise analysis as yet, but demography could be one reason why India's savings rate is going up.)

A higher savings rate should normally mean a higher investment rate as well. India's economy has grown despite a modest investment rate. Unlike China or the rest of East Asia, India has been a modest accumulator of capital (but has used it with greater care). The demographic transition could change one facet of the country's economic model, pushing up savings, and investment. If that happens, India will resemble its neighbors in East Asia more closely than before. From here, it is not very difficult to quickly calculate the impact on economic growth. India has traditionally had an incremental capital-output ratio of four. It produces one unit of new output for every four units of additional capital. An investment rate of 25% has thus led to a GDP growth rate of around 6% in recent years. If the demographic transition helps to push up the investment rate to close to 40% (without even considering foreign borrowings and investment, which too could be substantial), economic growth should spike to a China-like 10% a year. And if population growth continues on its current path and drops to 1% by 2015, average incomes will double every eight years compared to every 18 years at present.

The global labor market too could change beyond all recognition because of India's changing demographics. Around 15 million Indians are expected to join the labor pool every year, from now to 2020. That is the same as Germany's entire workforce. After 2020, India's population too will gradually start aging. So there is a 15-year window when the working population will peak as a percentage of the total population. India will have to capture its golden chance. To do so, there is some hard work to be done — *now*. The demographic dividend is not like some free gift lying in the mail. It has to be earned. Besides the larger issues of continued economic and institutional reforms, there are two main issues that will have to be sorted out. First, there should be an efficient financial sector in place that can collect these extra savings and direct them into productive economic activity. It is easy to fritter away capital in showpiece projects. Second, India can reap its demographic dividend only if the millions entering the working age are educated and skilled and hence able to add value. It would be no use if you have millions of new workers but have not given them the skills to do productive jobs. For now, let us focus on what is happening as far as education and skill levels of Indians go. There are actually a few pleasant surprises here.

CLASS STRUGGLE AND A SILENT REVOLUTION

India has close to a million schools, three times the number that was there when the country became independent in 1947. Every morning, around 200 million children from around the country go to these schools. Some go to fashionable schools in chauffeured cars while the vast majority goes by bus, bullock cart, bicycle, boat, and on foot. It is not easy going for kids. In the mountainous regions of Ladakh, at the northern tip of the country, for example, children have to sit on primitive wooden swings that are carried across deep gorges by pulleys and they then trudge a few kilometers up steep mountainsides to finally get to their classrooms. Others have to walk miles over dusty roads.[3] Sadly, 40 million or so children do not make this daily journey to school. They constitute a huge educational underclass that has been denied one of the basic rights of a modern and civilized society.

One of the biggest failures of the Indian Republic has been its inability to ensure that every child goes to school. This is compounded manifold when one considers the fact that the Republic's fundamental document — the Constitution — had declared way back in 1950, in one of the Directive Principles of State Policy, that "the State shall endeavour to provide, within a period of ten years ... for free and compulsory education for all children until they complete the age of fourteen years."[4] Then, in 2002, the Eighty-sixth Amendment to the Constitution actually made the right to education a Fundamental Right that is justiciable. Even so, 50 years after the original pious declaration, according to the 2001 census, India had an abysmal literacy rate of 65%, one of the lowest in the world. So 35 out of every 100 Indians cannot read and write. It is still a great advance over the 1940s, when less than a fifth of all Indians were literate. However, the current literacy rate is clearly inadequate in our times because it severely restricts the ability of one in every three Indians to participate in the global economy. Even more importantly, a huge illiterate population is a blot on a democratic society.

There are initial signs that the educational crisis is easing. School enrollments and attendance are rising swiftly in all corners of the country, in tandem with rising incomes and smaller family sizes. The attendance figures are the more important trend, because enrollment numbers are totted up at the beginning of every academic year; they often camouflage the fact that some kids drop out in the course of that year. Nearly 80% of all children between six and 10 years were attending school in 1999. Attendance is likely to have gone up further since then. Here is a quiet revolution that has escaped public attention.

What is especially pleasing is the fact that school attendance and literacy levels are improving where they matter the most. India has traditionally had a huge gender gap in education. Girls are far less likely to attend school than boys. This gender gap has started to narrow. Literacy rates for young girls between six and 10 years of age went up by 14% within six short years, between 1992 and 1998. Similarly, some of the states that lagged in education are catching up. Rajasthan and Madhya Pradesh saw literacy rates go up by 20% in the same period (Madhya Pradesh has since been bifurcated into two states). Overall, literacy rates increased faster between 1991 and 2001 than in any other previous decade since they were first tabulated in 1881.

Yet, there are problems as well. The story of one Indian girl tells us a lot about how difficult it often is to get even a basic school education in India and also how educational aspirations are rising in India.

ONE GIRL'S QUEST FOR EDUCATION

Unicef recently put a young Indian girl called Lalita Kumari on the cover of its flagship report — *The State of The World's Children 2004*. Her story is also recounted on the Unicef website. Lalita lives in Bihar, one of India's poorest states and one where gender rights are virtually absent. In her district, two-thirds of the people live below the poverty line and only one in four women is literate.

Her parents wanted to marry her off at ten, but Lalita attended a local girls' school without telling them. Her twin brother once caught her in school and beat her up. A girl's place is supposed to be the kitchen rather than the classroom. Her parents said nothing. Lalita decided to defy her parents and attended an innovative eight-month literacy program in her village. She also learned karate. Today, she runs a tailoring shop and teaches karate. She even went to New Delhi to help launch the report worldwide. Her parents are now proud of her.[5]

In Lalita's case it was the struggle of one brave girl against her family. Not every child has to stand up to parental opposition. Most children are luckier than Lalita. Families are sending their children to school with enthusiasm. Girls who want to stay in school face less parental opposition that before. In fact, Madhav Chavan of *Pratham*, a non-profit organization that works in the field of primary education, told me something interesting. In some areas of Mumbai, he said, the gender divide could actually be reversing. In some poor Muslim localities, parents are more likely to pull their sons out of school and send them to work to supplement family incomes. Daughters, on the other hand, are kept in school to "protect" them from outside society.[6]

This may be a stray example. There are other issues too, which cannot be glossed over. Most of the education surveys in India are based on self-assessments. Respondents are asked whether they are literate and the surveyors take them at their word. Many education activists insist that a large proportion of "literate" Indians cannot read, write, or do simple sums. These are significant criticisms. Yet, the rise in literacy and school attendance figures points to a great demand for education in India. That is the good news. The bad news is that the supply side response has been awfully inadequate.

THE TRUANT TEACHER

Though private schools are mushrooming rapidly across the nation, even in the poorest slums and hamlets, most of India's educational infrastructure is still in the public sector. Much of it consists of rundown schools that lack even basic facilities like toilets and drinking water. That is the next challenge. In February and March 1994, economist Jean Dreze and his colleagues conducted a field investigation on the state of government schools in Uttar Pradesh, India's most populous state. What they saw is a shocking testimony to the tattered state of the education system. Most school buildings were dilapidated. In one village, a local landlord had converted a school building into a cattle shed. In another, the teacher had made part of the school his home. In many villages, the furniture had been stolen by the village headman, the teacher, or some another influential person.[7]

Teacher absenteeism is another chronic problem. In India, especially in the poorer parts that are more dependent on government schools, it is the teacher who is more likely to play truant. About a quarter of teachers in India are likely to be absent on any given day. In the two worst states, Bihar and Jharkhand, absenteeism goes up to 38% and 42%, respectively. Teachers have walked away from their responsibilities in the very areas they are most needed. When you add the rising attendance figures with the high levels of teacher truancy the picture you get is not a pretty one. In general, children want to learn but there are not enough committed teachers to pull them out of illiteracy. Efficient delivery of social services is one of modern India's biggest challenges, and the state of schooling is to my mind the most damaging failure.

The response of the government has been typical — good intentions and the attempt to throw more money at the problem. On the intentions side, two initiatives are the most noteworthy. In 2001, the government launched the Sarva Shiksha Abhiyan (SSA), literally "a movement for education to all". The SSA's immediate target is to ensure universal education from the first to the fifth grade by 2007 and to ensure universal education till grade eight by 2010. In 2005, a Free and Compulsory Education Bill was also tabled in Parliament. One of the stated aims of the new left-of-center government is to double spending on education — from 3% to 6% of GDP. A small educational cess has been imposed on all taxes to fund this extra expenditure.

Will a bigger education budget do the trick? Look at the chart below. India has been a middling spender on education; yet educational outcomes are mediocre. This suggests that illiteracy cannot be removed quickly by merely throwing more money at the problem. A lot of attention has also to be given to the way the money is spent. The poor Indian is yearning for a decent education. The problem is with the education system (Table 4).

Table 4
A Poor Report Card

Country	Percent of illiterate adult population (2000)	Public expenditure on education (% of GNP)
India	44.2	3.2
China	15.0	2.3
Thailand	4.4	4.8
Indonesia	13.0	1.4
Sri Lanka	8.4	3.4
Bangladesh	59.2	2.2

Source: Ministry Of Human Resource Development, Government of India; http://www.education.nic.in.

FOOD FOR THOUGHT

Increased government spending on education could address some of the more serious infrastructure issues. For example, around 900,000 new classrooms are likely to be built over the next couple of years. Sceptics have good reason to ask whether all this will not mean more money down the drain, as is so often the case with social programs in India. In contrast, it is innovative and commonsense initiatives that have worked well in India.

The state of Tamil Nadu introduced a pioneering mid-day meal scheme for school children in the 1970s. It is one of the most successful social programs in poor countries. Children are provided a basic lunch at school. The government picks up the bill. A free lunch at school was an incentive for poor parents to send their children to school. When the then director of education in Tamil Nadu put forward the scheme, it was for giving a free meal on school days. The chief minister replied: "The director of education forgets that though schools do not function on Saturdays and Sundays, the stomach functions on all seven days." The mid-day meal scheme was made even more attractive because it was used on holidays as well.[8]

The success of the mid-day meal scheme in Tamil Nadu shows how incentives can work very well in education. Indian culture is full of stories that link learning and hunger. One of the earliest is in the *Chhandogya Upanishad*. Shwetaketu was the son of

Aruni. He mastered the holy books at a very young age, but also became arrogant about his intellectual abilities. His father decided to teach him a lesson. He told his son to go without food for seven days. He asked the arrogant boy to recite the holy books on the seventh day of his fast. The boy had forgotten everything. The point of this delightful story is obvious. You cannot learn on a hungry stomach. The mid-day meal scheme takes this simple insight and converts it into effective public policy.

Money needs to be spent intelligently and its use has to be monitored by the public authorities. How can this be done? There will perhaps never be one overarching answer to this question. A whole host of suggestions have been thrown into the policy cauldron. In one experiment, village children were given tamper-proof cameras that show the date on which a picture is taken. They were asked to take a photograph of their teacher every day. Salaries can then be linked to attendance (of the teachers, that is!). A few civil society organizations and technology companies are trying to use modern digital technology to provide quality education to areas that are starved of good teachers. Liberal educationists believe the way forward is through a system of education vouchers. Children can choose their schools and thus introduce an element of competition in what is now largely an inefficient state monopoly. And private entrepreneurs are trying to profit from the demand-supply mismatch by setting up for-profit schools, even in the poorest parts of India. The new education guarantee bill too has one interesting suggestion. Teachers are now recruited in a state cadre and they can be transferred to another part of a state after a few years. So it is difficult for individual communities to monitor them. One way out is to attach teachers to individual schools, which will ensure that they cannot ignore their jobs in a few years and move on to another school.

Santu is a girl of 13 living in Ranwasi village in the desert state of Rajasthan. Here's her story.

"I joined school at six. Although my parents were not literate, they were keen to educate me. I was also an eager learner. And I would never miss school. But slowly, I realised that I couldn't continue. Most of the time, teachers were absent. When they did come, they were hardly interested in teaching. Often, we would reach school, play in the ground, fight with one another and go back without even a single lesson. Also, I was beaten up every now and then because I wouldn't put up with neglect and humiliation. One teacher was particularly hostile to me because I came from a lower caste family. He would ask me to sit in the last row on the cold, bare floor, drink water from a separate pitcher, etc. In spite of such hurts, I continued school for four years hoping to be educated. But one day I had to quit. I had made a mistake, I had insisted on asking a question when the class was supposed to be silent. For that I was asked to stand outside the classroom through the day. It was very hot but nobody took any notice of my suffering and humiliation. I stopped going to school.

A few days later, the teacher came home to take me back to school because he feared a decrease in enrollment in his class. My parents sent me back. But he seemed even more hostile than before. He would hit me, and I would take it out on others. So I would be thrashed even more. I was falling behind in my studies, I had no motivation or sense of achievement. Finally, before the Class V exams, I quit."[9]

Santu's story is a vivid depiction of the growing dichotomy in India — children who want to go to school and teachers who refuse to do their jobs.

A YOUNG COUNTRY IN AN AGING WORLD

Perhaps it is the diet of sushi and sake that does the trick, but Japan has more than 25,000 centenarians. That is one centenarian for every 5,000 Japanese. The club is growing very fast. In 1963, there were only 163 Japanese men and women over the age of a hundred. The number grew to 1,000 in 1981 and 10,000 in 1998. The number of centenarians in Japan is growing at over 10% a year. The island of Okinawa has the highest concentration of centenarians in Japan (and the world). It is no wonder that demographers and diet gurus visit the area with religious reverence.[10] There is a reason why the growing number of centenarians in Japan makes its way into a book on the Indian economy. The world is aging, as people have fewer children and live longer. This is what one writer calls an "agequake". An earthquake destroys homes and office blocks; the agequake will tear down many of today's economic and social assumptions. The social security schemes in many Western nations are expected to become unsustainable when the baby-boomer generation that came into the world after World War II starts retiring in a few years. Dependency ratios will rise steeply. The population in many countries will start falling, and there will be fewer and fewer young men and women to work in farms, factories, and offices. A shortage of young workers could send wage rates higher and higher, thus making it uneconomic for the rich countries to produce a variety of essential goods and services. The division of labor across the globe is likely to acquire new dimensions. Low-value work could then be moved to countries where there is a large working population and wage rates are modest. This could be India's big opportunity — a wave of outsourcing that could make the current one look like a little ripple in a pool.

Japan is the most noteworthy case of a modern society that is threatened by an aging population. There will be an estimated 127 million Japanese in 2007. Then the number will start dropping. By 2050, there will be only 100 million Japanese. Many of them will be too old to work so the working population will drop at a faster rate than the total population. In effect, Japan will have 30 million fewer workers in 2050 than it has today. Other countries that are likely to report falling populations over the next few decades are Germany, Italy, Spain, Sweden, and Greece. It does not mean that these countries are going to be trapped in some variant of a permanent great depression. Fewer workers may not necessarily mean a lower output if they have more machines to work with. Some countries will adjust by changing the nature of work. People will work longer into their lives and perhaps in more flexible ways. Immigration is one other solution, but that will require a huge cultural transition, especially in an insular society such as Japan.

Meanwhile, even China will have to grapple with a prematurely aging population. Most countries see their fertility rates drop as they reach prosperity. China's communist government decrees that couples cannot have more than one child. As a result, the average age in China has gone up steadily. One in every ten Chinese is already over the age of 60, which is the rough indicator used to identify aging societies. By 2025, China will have 280 million senior citizens (or 18.4% of the population).

"With a large and fast-growing group of senior citizens, China, unfortunately, doesn't have an economy as well developed as Western countries had when they became aging societies. Compared to the $5,000–10,000 per-capita GDP of Western countries when they confronted the aging problem, China's per-capita GDP only reached $1,000 last year. China is a country getting old before getting rich" (Li Rongxia in the *Beijing Review*).[11]

THE DEMOGRAPHIC DIVIDEND

India will be spared the pressure of an aging society for a few more decades. It will have a young population for at least a couple of more decades. This will push up rates of domestic savings, investment, and economic growth. It will also hasten the shift of many types of jobs to India. The bulge in the working-age population and a revolution in primary education can also alter India's economic strategy, which has been built on modest investments and a focus on services. The spread of primary education will mean that the poor become more active participants in the global economy. Some of India's most stunning successes in recent years have come about because of low wages for everyone from engineers to accountants. Demographic change could stand the economic strategy of the 1990s on its head. Deutsche Bank economist Sanjeev Sanyal says:

> "The future is not about the infinite supply of cheap white-collar workers that is envisioned in the popular view. Instead, we feel that the future trajectory of growth will rely less on ... high-tech skills and more on (the) ability to absorb a mass mobilization of capital and low-skill workers."[12]

As urban wages increase, cost arbitrage in services will become less attractive. That's when India's silent millions will capture the headlines, but only if they have been given a decent education.

Demographic change will play a key role in India's economic transformation, but only if it is managed well. Let us not shut our eyes to the other possibility — a huge army of unskilled and unproductive Indians giving vent to an outburst of frustration. That is why the silent revolution in education is so important. It helps millions take the first step toward participation in the global economy.

NOTES

1. Data available at: http://www.censusindia.net.
2. "Why India Can Grow at Seven Percent or More: Projections and Reflections", by Dani Rodrik and Arvind Subramanian, IMF Working Paper, July 2004.
3. *Going to School in India*, Penguin India, 2003.
4. *The Constitution of India*, Universal Law Publishing Company, 2001, p. 94
5. *The State of The World's Children 2004*, Unicef, 2004.
6. In an interview with the author.
7. *Indian Development: Selected Regional Perspectives*, edited by Jean Dreze and Amartya Sen, Delhi: Oxford University Press, 1997.
8. Letter by K. Venkatsubramanian, member of the Tamil Nadu Planning Commission, *Business Line*, June 14, 2004.
9. *The Little Magazine*, Vol. VI, Nos. 1–2, 2004.
10. Some of these data are from an article in *Japan Times*, September 14, 2005.
11. "China: An Aging Society", *Beijing Review*, available at: http://www.bjreview.com.cn.
12. "India: From White Collar to Blue", by Sanjeev Sanyal, *Deutsche Bank*, October 19, 2005.

Chapter 4

India Calling

SUCCESS IN BITS AND BYTES

Modern airports tend to be sanitized and soulless monstrosities, but they are often a great place to observe the global economy at work. The elves of our age rush in and out of the duty-free shops, on their way to the next flight, the next project, the next meeting. You would have been hard-pressed to find an Indian in this rising tide of business vagabonds till about a decade ago. Today, in contrast, you could not miss them however hard you tried. You will always find a group of Indian engineers waiting for their connecting flight in one of the great clearing-houses of modern international travel — for example, London, Amsterdam, Frankfurt, Singapore, or Hong Kong. They will be there, lugging their laptops as they make their way from one terminal to the other. In all likelihood, they will be part of the only industry where India is at (or very near) the top of the global heap — software services.

The writers of software code have been the earliest builders of the great Indian outsourcing juggernaut. But others have also come on board subsequently — from call center workers taking complaints from harried customers many time zones away to an army of scientists testing the latest drug or designing the latest computer chip. I was once sitting in a restaurant in Mumbai late at night, when I noticed a cauldron of accents bubbling at the table behind mine. There was everything from the East End cockney to the Mid-western twang. It was not a tourist group enjoying its beer, but a gang of young call center workers comparing notes, between giggles, on how to deal with customers from different parts of the world.

At the other end of the outsourcing spectrum, top-notch engineers and scientists work in innovation shops set up by around 150 major global companies including some of the world's most high-profile companies such as Intel, Microsoft, and Nokia. Microsoft, for example, already employs 4,000 people in India in two research labs; that number will go up by another 3,000 in the next four years, more than in any other country (outside the US). And in between, there are radiologists checking X-rays of patients in the United States, accountants helping Britons file their tax returns and editors proof-reading scientific journals from Europe (Table 5).

Table 5
The Beneficiaries Of Offshoring

India	12.2
Ireland	8.6
Canada	3.8
Mexico	0.5
Latin America	1.8
Israel	3.6
South Africa	0.1
Eastern Europe	0.6
Russia	0.3
China	3.4
Philippines	1.7
Thailand	0.1
Other Asia	2.3
Australia	0.4

Source: McKinsey & Co. (2002)

THE NEW ECONOMICS OF TRADE

How does one explain the rise of outsourcing, from a marginal activity in the global economy as recently as in the 1980s, to one of the central policy concerns of today? Services such as credit card processing or airline bookings were once believed to be "non-tradable." Consumers of these services were slaves of distance: they had to buy them some place close to home. You had to go to a local hospital to get a medical opinion and the accountant down the street helped you with your tax filings. You could not just get the job done by someone sitting a few thousand miles away. The transport costs would be prohibitive.

Traditionally, a service was likely to be traded only if its price differential in two countries was more than the cost of traveling between the two countries. This sort of trade is still seen now and then. Take the booming business of medical tourism. The US citizens and Europeans who cannot afford expensive surgeries at home fly down to countries like India, Thailand, and South Africa to get their bodies mended. The cost of an airline ticket is far less than the savings achieved by getting operated on in a country with cheap doctors and hospitals.

Medical tourism entails movement of the consumers, rather than that of goods and services. There are also the rare instances when the producer or provider moves across international borders to service his customer, as when a famous surgeon flies to another country to take a look at his patient. The movement of warm bodies is always going to be a fringe activity. So, while global trade in hard stuff like wheat and cars grew explosively after the end of the Second World War, trade in services was modest. The markets for radiologists and accountants remained resolutely local. They could not be outsourced to countries such as India.

Two factors helped push services towards globalization. At one end, many services are prone to persistent inflation because there is little scope for productivity gains. Their prices rise faster than the general rate of inflation, especially in rich countries with high wages. Economist William Baumol called this the cost disease. He once illustrated his case with the example of orchestral music. Orchestras (or barbers for that matter) experience little or no labor-saving innovation.

"A Haydn symphony written to be performed by 30 musicians and lasting one-half an hour will require 15 person hours of human labor for an "authentic" performance, no less than it did at the end of the 18th century. But elsewhere in the economy it takes less and less labor every year to produce a product. The amount of labor needed to produce an automobile declines more than three percent each year, on the average. This means that if wages rise at more or less the same rate in car production and in orchestras, then clearly, the cost per performance must rise faster than the cost per car, because in car production rising wages are offset by the reduced use of labor per car, while in orchestras there are few such offsets. Thus, orchestra costs are condemned to rise every year, cumulatively, at a rate faster than the average of the economy's prices; in other words, faster than the rate of inflation"(Baumol).[1]

The cost disease creates an excellent case for cost saving through international trade. An autoworker in Japan can still compete with a peer in China by rolling out more cars per hour. A cello player in Paris cannot become more productive by using better machines or management techniques. Haydn symphonies remain non-tradable partly because of quality issues: would you substitute the great Vienna Philharmonic Orchestra with a cheaper version? But what about other services where quality can be equalized fairly easily? These services can be bought from other countries — that is, outsourced.

It is — or was — easier said than done, however, because sending a tax filing to an accountant in faraway India would have meant putting a stack of papers into an envelope, sending it by FedEx and, perhaps, following up with an expensive international phone call. It was costly, in terms of both time and money. Then came the digital revolution. Suddenly these non-tradables became tradable across great distances. Anything that could be digitized and sent across wires was fair game. Wages in India were often a tenth of what they were for similar work in the United States and Europe. One way to escape the cost disease was to send work to places where labor was cheap.

Some services are still protected. Barbers in the United States, for example, are safe since their work cannot be done across wires — at least for now, since new technologies that allow surgeons to conduct operations across continents may some day be used in barber shops; some day, perhaps, oilmen in Dallas will get their locks clipped by barbers sitting thousands of miles away in India. Anyway, work can now be sent to places where labor is efficient and cheap. The telecom revolution did to the Indian outsourcing industry what the invention of the faster steamships did to agricultural exports from Australia and Argentina a hundred years ago. Transport costs collapsed and the world's richest markets were no longer out of bounds.

COMPUTERS AND KARMA

India has consistently topped the list of great outsourcing destinations in recent years. An army of engineers, the widespread use of English in the country, low wages and (since the late 1990s) a reasonably good telecom system has ensured that the Indian outsourcing industry has been on steroids. Software has been the early triumph. From very modest beginnings in the late 1960s and early 1970s, the Indian software services industry has grown by leaps and bounds — from $12 million in 1980 to $12 billion less than 25 years later.

Many countries — from Mexico to China — are now trying to learn from the Indian outsourcing story. The attempt may be worthwhile, but the task is more complicated than is commonly assumed. Looking back, it is easy to fit what happened into neat patterns and then try to copy these patterns. Votaries of industrial policy and the nurturing of national champions (and every country has them by the hundreds) may then try to build domestic outsourcing industries by official fiat. There is a cautionary note to be added here. There was no secret mantra that a few far-sighted national planners in India repeatedly chanted to create a tech miracle. India's outsourcing success was never planned. It was the result of a sweet mix of ability and luck, of public policy and entrepreneurial vision. Nobody set out to create a multibillion dollar winner. It was an accidental revolution.

Cultural determinists would be tempted to argue that India's success in software is almost preordained. Ancient India's greatest contribution to mathematics is the zero, given to us by the great 7th century mathematician Bramhagupta. Pingala, a musicologist in India's grand classical age, is said to have devised a binary system to explain the various musical notes. And modern computer software is written in a binary system of zeros and ones. So there is an invisible karmic thread linking ancient gurus and modern geeks. India is naturally suited to dominate a digitized world of zeros and ones. Get it?

While this line of thought is attractive, the origins of India's success in computer software are far more recent and pedestrian. The first computer to arrive in India was a Hollerinth Electronic Computer HEC-2M. It came just a few years after the world's first computer was created in 1946 at the University of Pennsylvania at Philadelphia. The HEC-2M was installed in 1956 at the Indian Statistical Institute in Kolkata, which had been established by P.C. Mahalanobis, a brilliant statistician, confidant of Jawaharlal Nehru and father of India's flawed five-year economic plans. Nehru, Mahalanobis and their band of national planners got several things wrong as far as economic policy goes, but there is one area where they cannot be faulted — their firm belief that India needed science and technology if it was to develop into a modern nation. That first computer used to process data was a link between India's scientific and economic aspirations.

The potential of computers to improve lives in a desperately poor country such as India was recognized very early on. The Indian government set up a Committee on Electronics way back in 1963. Its chairman was Homi Bhabha, a fine nuclear physicist and the father of India's very successful atomic program. The Committee on Electronics set up a working group on computers headed by a physicist named R. Narasimhan. This working group's report in 1968 was almost prophetic in the way it mapped the future.

> "A computer system is only as versatile as the software that is made available with it…. Software is business. Software is strategic. Thus it would be very foolhardy if a programme for the manufacture of the computer systems … does not have built into it a programme for a scheme for the development of appropriate software … software development can be farmed out to other organizations … this is also a labour-intensive activity except that it requires intellectually skilled manpower…. Software development would seem to have very high employment potential in a country like India … the export potential, as well as the value added in the case of software, is very large."

Almost every major theme in India's remarkable software success story is anticipated in this passage.[2]

The more controversial issue is how the government tried to convert vision to reality. It was one thing to see the future and another thing to get there. How did India do it? One of the enduring myths about India's stunning success in software is that it came about without the backing of public policy. This is just not true. Enterprise did not operate in a vacuum. It never does. Public policy did play an important part as well, right from those early committees and their far-sighted reports till more recent attempts at encouragement through tax breaks and the setting up of special software export zones. That is textbook stuff. But, and this is where the story is interesting, public policy helped spark off India's stunning software boom in some perverse ways as well.

The law of unintended consequences played its strange tricks. Policies that had other objectives helped the nascent software business grow. Curiously, a few cases of government action that would definitely be denounced as huge mistakes by today's reigning economic consensus also helped. There are many whimsical twists and turns in the plot that few seem to be aware of.

OOPS! UNINTENDED CONSEQUENCES

The Indian policy establishment's early attempts to promote a domestic tech industry were in line with similar attempts to promote capabilities in other areas such as steel and engineering. The thrust was on protectionist policies and creating public-sector giants. The government tried to promote national champions in the 1960s. The Electronics Corporation of India Ltd. (ECIL) was set up in 1967 to build hardware and write software. These early attempts at building tech companies in the public sector met with limited success. Import tariffs were sky-high — 135% on hardware and 100% of software. India's cost advantage in labor was negated by high tariffs. Bank finance was not available, since Indian banks in those day took inventories as collateral before extending working capital; a software company does not have any physical inventory to offer as collateral. Multinational corporations (MNCs) were also discouraged, thus preventing the flow of the latest knowledge into India.

All these policies effectively ensured that software development work did not come to India in the late 1960s and early 1970s. So, in what now seems a natural reaction, Indian programmers were forced to go abroad to work on projects. Thus was born the body shopping business. India's first software companies were entangled in a web of restrictions. They gained their first contracts by shipping cheap labor abroad. Tight controls on the inflow of capital and knowledge were met with an outflow of labor.

In 1973, F.C. Kohli visited the United States as director of the Institute of Electrical and Electronic Engineers. His day job was managing director of Tata Consultancy Services (TCS), a division of Tata Sons, the holding company of one of India's largest business conglomerates. TCS was set up in 1968. Its first job was to manage punch card operations at Tisco, itself a steel company of the Tata group. A year later, TCS was asked to computerize the inter-branch reconciliation work of the Central Bank of India. It did the job well, and got orders from 14 other banks. Yet, revenues in the early days were not enough to profitably employ the company's first employees — 10 consultants and 200 punch card operators.

Such were the modest beginnings of an industry that was to generate heated debates in a US presidential election more than three decades later. So, it was 1973 and Kohli was in the United States. He made a detour to Detroit and visited the offices of Burroughs (then the second largest computer hardware manufacturer after IBM). An Indian software company got its first outsourcing contract. A little later, TCS got an order from the Institutional Group and Information Company (IGIC), a data center servicing 10 banks and around two million customers. Of course, these early contracts were for "body shopping." TCS shipped cheap Indian technical labor to the United States to get the jobs done.

There were some attempts to encourage software companies to do part of their jobs in India. The Department of Electronics had put out newspaper advertisements in 1970, calling for proposals from Indian companies to make software for the export market. The response was tepid. However, in 1973, a special export zone was set up in Santa Cruz, a Mumbai suburb, to house software shops.

The big push, however, came in 1977 when IBM decided to exit India. A law passed in 1973 had restricted foreign ownership in any company operating in India to 40%. Big Blue operated through a 100% subsidiary, and it was in no mood to bring its stake down to the regulatory maximum. It decided to leave.

The decision to force MNCs like IBM and Coca Cola out of the country was clearly unwarranted. But what was otherwise a foolish decision acted as a catalyst for India's software industry. It created space for domestic companies to take root and grow. In 1981, seven engineers who worked for Patni Computers, a domestic firm that was a reseller for computers made by US firm Data General, walked out and started Infosys Technologies with a capital of Rs. 10,000. The early days of companies such as Infosys were tough. There were strict controls on the import of computers. Companies had to prove that they would earn foreign exchange by using these computers. Even after an import license was procured, import tariffs were sky-high.

"Although all its revenues came from foreign markets, Infosys had neither the capacity to incur the cost of purchasing and maintaining its own computer in India nor the space to house such a computer. Its solution to this dilemma was one that is characteristic of its founders' ingenuity in making do with scarce resources. It purchased the computer and had it installed on the premises of a major customer in India. It then bartered its technical knowledge with computer time and at the same time used the computer to train new employees and develop products."

This example is used in a case study on Infosys written for the students of the Wharton Business School at the University of Pennsylvania.[3] Notice the fact that all this had to be done for *one* computer. It gives us some idea of how bad the roadblocks were at the high noon of Indian socialism. All this started changing later in the 1980s. In 1984, India got a new prime minister, Rajiv Gandhi. He was the first national leader who had come of age after the country became independent, and so was free of a lot of the old socialist ideological baggage. Rajiv instinctively realized that India needed modern technology and a reformed economy. He was surrounded by a group of technocrat friends, who were dubbed his computer boys by his opponents.

Rajiv's government introduced a new computer policy in 1985, within three weeks of coming to power. Import duties on hardware were brought down to 60%. Export revenues were exempt from tax in 1985. And Texas Instruments started a small operation in Bangalore in 1986, with 15 people working on chip design. It saw India's potential as an outsourcing destination much before most of its peers. It decided to set up its own earth station in 1987 and was encouraged to do so by the young and reforming prime minister. This direct satellite link between India and the United States changed the rules of the game. The physical transfer of either programmers or floppies to the United States was no longer necessary. Software could be beamed between the two countries.

BANKERS AND GEEKS

Meanwhile, there was another lucky break. Around this time, the Reserve Bank of India (RBI), the central bank, decided that domestic banks should start computerizing their operations. It appointed a committee headed by deputy governor C. Rangarajan to advise banks how to go about wiring their processes. The Rangarajan committee asked banks to use systems based on the UNIX software platform. UNIX was then not seen as a very sophisticated operating system in Western countries. The government put out a tender for 400 UNIX systems. The market was large, and Indian software companies trained their engineers to work with UNIX. They thus learned the skills that were in great demand in the United States and Europe in the 1990s.

The industry took off in that decade, with the spread of globalization and the telecom revolution. India too opened up its telecom sector in 1994. Software exports rocketed. The Y2K scare also helped. There was a fear that the infamous millennium bug (which was expected to confuse computers between the years 2000 and 1900 and thus make them impotent) would force everything from computers to markets to airplanes to crash. Indian programmers were called in by a panicky world to set the problem right. Suddenly, they landed everywhere. Once they got the job done, it was relatively easy to get other contracts from grateful clients. The Y2K scare helped Indian software companies get their foot in the doors of global companies.

What I have recounted above is not a comprehensive history of India's software industry. It is very selective and a bit of a whistle-stop tour through recent economic history. Yet, the important point is that India's success in software was not planned by a group of strategists pouring over spreadsheets in air-conditioned offices. There was no grand plan, no blueprint that other countries can now copy. Many factors helped — public policy, enterprise, and sheer luck. Technology is often seen as the ultimate Schumpeterian industry — driven by heroic entrepreneurs and prone to gales of creative destruction. Yet, government action too has played an important part in many tech success stories, from the growth of minicomputers (a fall-out of the US space program), to the internet (which was built for the US defense establishment) to the Indian software triumphs (where a combination of visionary and misguided national policies were the initial catalysts). The story of India's success in outsourcing is far more complicated than is commonly realized. Even the notorious tech bubble of the 1990s helped.

OH! WHAT A BEAUTIFUL BUBBLE

Hermann Goering famously said that he reached for his gun whenever he heard the word culture uttered around him. There are many pundits today who would like to do something similar when they hear the word dot-com. It is more than five years since the dot-com dream collapsed under its own weightlessness. Yet, the pain lingers on.

It is the wont of bubbles to pop some day. When they do, they inevitably leave behind a big mess. So getting worked up about the great technology madness of the late 20th century is an effortless sport. It is thus easy to rage against the dot-com madness of the late 1990s, the unbelievable valuations that companies with no hope of earning profits were awarded, the sheer greed and financial gluttony. But even the most profligate era has its genuine achievements. The unlamented tech bubble of the late 1990s is no exception to this rule.

Though the word bubble is often used very loosely these days, it is normally used to describe a market or an economy where prices have run ahead of reality. Galloping asset prices attract the investor hordes. They participate in a buying frenzy that drives down the price of capital. Cheap money has its risks, but it also makes life easier, not just for crooks but also for genuine entrepreneurs. People are ready to take more risks and back new technologies. It is convenient to remember only half the story after a bubble blows up in your face. And let us face it — some good work does get done in such times.

Many countries have, over the decades, taken advantage of investment manias to build up their physical infrastructure (e.g. roads, ports, and railways). It could be the United States in the 1880s or Thailand in the 1990s. The mad desire to own a piece of the "unprofitable" action sends capital rushing into areas where cautious investment angels fear to tread. The investors often lose their shirts and sarongs, but others gain from their bouts of overconfidence. The tech bubble did something similar to the telecom infrastructure — and one of the unexpected beneficiaries of the reckless investment in telecom networks was the Indian software sector. There were investors ready to back projects that would have seemed insane in calmer times. Putting money in infrastructure, be it a road or an undersea cable, is tricky because these investments are lumpy. Large chunks of capital have to be committed on day one. Also, payback times are very long. Investors have good reason to be wary. It takes a bubble to draw them out of their comfort zones.

Prices of computer hardware had started falling since the early 1980s. Computer use spread rapidly, which was good news for software providers. As the 1990s progressed, more and more companies started outsourcing part of their software work to India. But telecom and bandwidth costs started falling only at the end of the decade, as telecom companies poured money into new optic fiber networks that would string the world together. This proved to be a godsend for companies that sent their products and services over these lines. A software company sending its code over a leased line to the United States or a call center taking hundreds of telephone calls from London every hour benefit greatly when transmission costs come down sharply. So, like IBM's decision in 1977 to leave India or the RBI's decision in 1987 to force banks to use UNIX as their software platform, the tech bubble of the 1990s proved to be a lucky break for the Indian software industry.

To borrow the terminology of the non-digital world, transport costs came down dramatically. The mad rush to invest in telecom networks was the digital equivalent of the opening of the Suez Canal. Trade was bound to explode.

In a survey of telecom that was published in October 2003, *The Economist* neatly explained what had happened.

> "In the four months from the beginning of 1998, says Andrew Odlyzko, a telecom guru at the University of Minnesota, the amount of fibre in the ground increased five-fold. Meanwhile, the technology of feeding signals into the fibres at one end and extracting them at the other end increased the transmission of each strand of fibre a hundred fold, so total transmission capacity increased 500-fold. But over the same period demand for transmission capacity merely quadrupled, a rise that could easily be accommodated by existing networks. Mr Odlyzko estimates that around $150 billion was spent building unnecessary telecoms networks in America and another $50 billion in other parts of the world."[4]

These $200 billion of investments in telecom networks may not have been raised if the white light of the internet revolution had not blinded investors. Undoubtedly, many of those who trusted the likes of World Com with their savings had to see their net worth wither away. But the one hard benefit that came out of this crazy episode is that the cost of an international telephone call collapsed. A call between Bangalore and San Francisco was no longer a luxury. Falling prices are good news for consumers, and among the consumers who benefited from falling telecom and bandwidth costs were India's burgeoning software and outsourcing companies.

OF CORN AND CALL CENTERS

For all the agony and ecstasy over the outsourcing of service jobs to countries like India and the Philippines, the actual numbers are quite modest. Less than a million Indians are employed in jobs that involve outsourced services. The number is growing very rapidly. Yet, it is unlikely that there will be more than 2.5 million Indians working in software companies, call centers, research labs and the like by 2010. The Indian labor market is about 200 times bigger. So what is the fuss about?

There will be many who will be quick to argue that 2.5 million may not seem like a lot of workers in a vast and well-populated country like India. But would not the impact on labor markets elsewhere be significant? Again, the numbers are not as large as some of the more vocal opponents of outsourcing suggest (often without any proof). Consulting firm McKinsey & Company estimated at the end of a research project in 2005 that the total offshore employment in services will reach 4.1 million, or around 1.2% of the total demand for service-sector jobs in the rich countries. Every year, far more jobs are lost because of other factors. Alliance Capital says that around 31 million jobs were eliminated in the world's 20 richest countries between 1995 and 2002. People lose jobs because of myriad reasons, and not all of them are related to international trade. Technological change and changes in consumer demand often push more people out of their existing jobs than factors related to trade and globalization. Yet, it is the latter that inevitably make it to the headlines and TV chat shows. Why?

There are two possible responses why politicians, TV hosts, and newspaper editors love to harp on about the costs of outsourcing. First, the loss of manufacturing jobs is seen as being almost inevitable, despite the occasional attempts by Western governments to protect their steel, auto, and textile industries. The employment structure of an economy changes in tune with its level of development — from agriculture to manufacturing to services. So while the loss of jobs in manufacturing is almost inevitable (and perhaps even desirable) in countries like the United States, the loss of jobs in software or biotech is more of an issue because it is said to undercut future competitiveness.

Second, while the number of service jobs that will move to India may not be as high as commonly believed, the effect on wages will be far more significant. The threat of outsourcing will be enough to keep a lid on wages. The young engineer in Silicon Valley will live in the knowledge that there is an equally bright young girl in Bangalore who will do his job for far less. The common belief that investment in education can help the rich countries protect their jobs is wrong. As I have explained at the beginning of this chapter, the key issue is not whether a service requires skills or not; it is whether the service can be traded digitally or not. A janitor in a New York hospital is better placed to survive outsourcing than a radiologist in the same hospital.

Outsourcing could even undermine the post-war social contract between capital and labor in many rich countries, especially those in Europe that have a strong welfare state. In an interview with the German newspaper *Der Spiegel*, Singapore's minister mentor Lee Kuan Yew framed the issue in his typically blunt and prescient way:

> "The social contract that led to workers sitting on the boards of companies and everybody being happy rested on this condition: I work hard, I restore Germany's prosperity, and you, the state, you have to look after me. I'm entitled to go to Baden Baden for spa recuperation one month every year. This old system was gone in the blink of an eye when two to three billion people joined the race — one billion in China, one billion in India and over half-a-billion in Eastern Europe and the former Soviet Union."[5]

The contentious issue is whether the break-up of the successful post-war social contract in the West will be all bad news. Or will some good come out of it? Actually, the outsourcing debate mirrors the concerns that were raised during earlier battles over free trade. The first major battle on free trade was over the Corn Laws, import tariffs that were introduced in Britain in 1825 in order to protect landowners and farmers from cheaper imported foodgrain. David Ricardo, the pioneering 19th century economist who showed how trade based on comparative advantage worked to benefit both importing and exporting countries, was one of those who fought against the Corn Laws, arguing that they would keep food prices high and force the British economy into stagnation. The Corn Laws were repealed in 1845, but the core of the debate keeps getting resurrected time and again.

Outsourcing is a new form of international trade, with all its attendant benefits. In a sense, the fracas over the outsourcing of services to India in the 21st century is very similar to the fight over the Corn Laws in 19th century England. As always, the key question is whether trade and specialization lead to greater productivity and incomes. And as always, the answer is yes. Let us stick with the world of computers for some time. Economist Robert Solow had quipped in the 1980s that we could see the effects of the computer revolution everywhere, except in the productivity statistics. For nearly a decade after that, economists battled with one another on the issue of whether the use of computers actually makes economies more productive. The debate is now being settled in favor of the computer enthusiasts.

One reason why productivity rose sharply in the 1990s was the widespread use of computers in factories, offices, and homes. The spread of computing, in turn, was partly due to the fall in hardware prices. While technology change was the main cause of falling computer prices, international trade helped too, as companies such as Dell started sourcing from cheaper Asian countries. Catherine Mann of the Institute of International Economics has estimated that globalization of computer manufacturing pushed down prices by between 10% and 30%. She argues that a similar globalization of software will push down software prices and unleash the next round of productivity in the United States.[6]

While the economies of rich countries are likely to benefit at the macro level from the globalization of services, there will always be individual losers. If it was the turn of the English farmers then, it could be the US software engineers now. How societies manage the loss of some types of jobs and how they retrain their workers has always been an important issue in modern economies, as they try to balance the twin needs of a dynamic economy and a stable society. The extent of the problem is still not clear today. Is it merely a question of retraining a few million workers? Or is it, as Lee Kuan Yew suggests, the beginning of the break-up of the post-war social contract in Europe and the United States? These questions will keep haunting policy makers in the West. Meanwhile, the benefits of outsourcing are far more clear in India. The debates here are of a quite different sort.

APPLAUSE AND BRICKBATS

Thousands of Europeans plan their annual holidays with the help of online travels firms like eBookers, a company founded by a Briton of Indian origin called Dinesh Dhamija. A lot of the drudge work at eBookers is sent to an Indian subsidiary called Technovate. That is what hundreds of other firms in Europe and the United States also do, but Technovate is an interesting example because about 10% of its staff comes from Europe. The reason is that while Indians are proficient in English, they lack exposure to other European languages. They are incapable of taking calls from French or Swedish customers with the same confidence with which they handle English-speaking customers. This is why a company like Technovate depends on young workers from some parts of Europe to man its desks.

Technovate is a special case. It gets in young Europeans because of language barriers. But it is not the only company that has attracted expatriate workers. One research company estimates that there will be 120,000 foreigners working in India's outsourcing companies by 2010. *Financial Times* reported the story of one such unlikely migrant worker in 2004. Jim Shell, a resident of Fort Worth in Texas, lost two jobs before he decided to move to India. He works in an outsourcing company called WNS — owned by private equity firm Warburg Pincus and British Airways — in Mumbai. There are many others like Shell who have come to India in search of work.[7]

Surprising as it may sound, India could be headed for a labor shortage in some parts of its economy. Hundreds of thousands of graduates come out of college every year, but not all of them have the requisite skills that outsourcing and software companies are looking for. Wages are rising, though they are still low by international standards. It is interesting that some Indian companies are setting up shop in cheaper markets such as China and the

Philippines. One of the biggest challenges in the next few years is to train people — either through the official education system or private training institutes or through in-house training by companies. These are the inevitable consequences of success.

On the other hand, the fact that workers from developed countries are ready to consider careers in India shows how far the country has traveled in recent years. The first men and women who went to the United States in the 1980s to get business for their software companies will tell you how difficult it was to sell the idea to US executives who saw India as no more than a poverty-ridden backwater. Indians ran motels in the United States and curry houses in Britain. Could they manage more complex business processes? In those early years, half the marketing presentation was often taken up by the need to sell India. Only then could the nuts and bolts of the business proposition be discussed. That has now changed. There is no need to sell India as an outsourcing destination. Just about everyone who matters knows about it. Meetings are now about more concrete issues — pricing, technical capability, and deliverables.

Despite its roaring success, the outsourcing industry in India has not been without its critics. At one end, there are the economic nationalists who dismiss it as nothing more than a collection of air-conditioned sweatshops doing the dumb work of global corporations. At the other end, less excitable minds are disturbed by the fact that this industry has few local linkages. Unlike an automobile company that creates jobs not just for its workers but also for car dealers, mechanics, and chauffeurs, an outsourcing company has no secondary impact on the economy.

Yet, despite these criticisms, what really matters is that the outsourcing success has done two things — it has told the rest of the world that India is no laggard and it has convinced Indians that they can compete in the global economy. The accomplishments of software companies such as Wipro, Infosys, and TCS have created ripples not just in the economy, but in society and politics as well. Here are companies that have grown at a blistering pace, have shared wealth with their employees and have maintained unimpeachable ethical standards. Furthermore, their promoters generously give away their personal wealth to support social causes like education, health, and urban regeneration.

It is a completely new paradigm for Indian companies as well as for Indian society at large. The outsourcing of software and other services is never going to be a dominant business in India — either in terms of GDP or employment. A million (or even three million) technologists are going to be like a drop in the nation's expansive labor ocean. But the success in outsourcing is still of immense importance because it has been like a vanguard, giving Indians the confidence that they too can go out and compete in the world.

NOTES

1. Quoted by http://www.truckandbarter.com on July 1, 2003.
2. Balaji Parthasarthy, *Iterations: an Interdisciplinary Journal of Software History*, May 3, 2004.
3. Available at: http://www.infosys.com.
4. Beyond The Bubble, a survey of telecoms by Tom Standage, *The Economist*, October 11, 2003.
5. *Der Spiegel*, October 8, 2005.
6. Catherine L. Mann, "Globalisation of IT Services and White Collar Jobs: The Next Wave of Productivity Growth", Institute of Economic Growth, International Economics Policy Briefs, December 2003.
7. *Financial Times*, July 8, 2004, by Khozem Merchant.

Chapter 5

The Global Agenda

Ranbaxy Laboratories is a pharmaceuticals company based in New Delhi and one of India's most successful multinationals. An Indian multinational is no longer an oxymoron. More than 70% of Ranbaxy's total revenue comes from its international operations. Just as the large software companies sell a greater part of their products and services outside India, so also does Ranbaxy have subsidiaries in many countries today, including the United States and China. It is one of the top ten sellers of generic drugs in the United States, third in Brazil and fifth in Britain. Its journey toward globalization is an interesting case study on how attitudes toward globalization have changed in India — both in government and within companies — over the past two decades or so.

India's tryst with globalization has gone through three distinct stages — an initial bout of fear, particularly just after the economy was opened up in 1991, then a resigned acceptance of the inevitable, and finally a belated discovery that globalization can be a blessing. The occasional paroxysms of fear of the foreigner do break out even today — as they do in most countries, including free-market bastions like the United States. The "enemy" could be anybody — US fast food companies that want to destroy Indian culinary culture, rapacious Chinese traders who dump their goods in this country with impunity, or hedge funds that have set out to shatter India's dreams. But these are, so to speak, like the occasional rashes on a healthy body. India is now more comfortable with the rest of the world than it ever was in recent history. Nowhere is this more valid than in India Inc.'s tortuous engagement with the world.

Ranbaxy was a small pharmaceutical company when it decided to look beyond the Indian market way back in the 1970s, when most Indian companies were quite content to hide behind huge tariff barriers and milk the domestic market. Ranbaxy's initial foray was into Nigeria in 1978. Four years later, it decided to move into Malaysia. D.S. Brar, who later became the CEO of the company but was then part of the middle management, was sent there to clear the way for a manufacturing plant. Brar visited the Malaysian Industry Development Authority (MIDA). His initial meetings there were an eye-opener. "What is your import tariff on the raw materials?" he asked an MIDA official. He was told that Ranbaxy would have to pay a 5% tax on its imported inputs. "What are your import tariffs on finished products?" Brar asked. The answer was the same: 5%.

There are two instructive cues here. First, Malaysia had low levels of import tariffs way back in 1982, when Indian industry was cosseted by import tariffs that often exceeded 100%. The official justification for this insane protection was that it would help local industry grow — the old infant industry argument. Toddlers need wise parental care. As in so many parts of the world, the infants soon descended into premature senility. The youthful zest that is needed to compete and grow was starkly absent in Indian industry. There was rampant inefficiency, as anybody who has had his bones rattled while sitting in an overpriced Ambassador car in the 1980s will testify. Protectionism came with a heavy cost for ordinary citizens. The record speaks for itself — Malaysia with low levels of import taxes and growing links with the rest of the world outpaced India for the next decade and more.

The second interesting issue that emerges from Brar's discussion with the Malaysian official is the structure of tariffs. They were the same on both the inputs and the finished product. One of the grand assumptions of Indian trade policy is that the tariffs on inputs should be lower than those on finished goods. It ostensibly helps local manufacture of value-added goods. Even today, this conviction persists and is cleverly used to lobby for subtle protection against cheaper imports. Malaysia was doing nothing of the sort. It was taxing the import of inputs and finished goods at the same rate. So when a surprised Brar told the MIDA official that his country was not giving any incentives for local manufacturing, he was repeating the conventional wisdom of the day in India. The Malaysian official replied:

> "If it is not viable and economical for you, please don't produce it. We are not asking you to produce. We will welcome industry but will not make industry inefficient in our country. You decide if it makes business sense to produce from raw materials and if it makes sense, please do so. If you feel imports of finished goods at five per cent is a better option, that is also your choice."[1]

Brar says that he was then in the Indian mindset. "I was made to look like a fool. But it made us think differently."[1] Ranbaxy went on to chart a stunning plan to become a global company. Significantly, it went out into the global market when most of Indian industry preferred the easy pickings in the domestic market. But there is more to this story than the discovery of a "eureka" moment for a wannabe multinational corporation (MNC), a larger and more important point. The agnosticism that Malaysia (and many other countries in Asia) showed between imports and local manufacturing helped maintain competitiveness and growth. They refused to make a fetish of local manufacture. The over-arching goal of policy was to maintain the competitiveness of the domestic industry. The benefits included faster growth for the economy and lower prices for consumers. The World Bank showed in a 1996 study how developed countries that had integrated into the world economy between 1984 and 1993 grew at 3% more a year than the closed economies. And the Asian Development Bank said in 1997 that the open economies in Asia had 2% higher growth rates between 1965 and 1990.

A lot has changed in India since that early meeting between an Indian manager and a Malaysian bureaucrat — both in government policy and corporate strategy. Much time was lost in the intervening period. Now, almost two decades after Ranbaxy and the earlier pioneers, many other Indian companies have started following in their footsteps. The result: the first few Indian multinationals are here. Finally.

A SMALL TOWN IN GERMANY

Ennepetal is a small town of about 33,000 people situated in the Ruhr, Germany's industrial heartland. The Ruhr is blessed with lavish deposits of coal, the fuel used by many sectors of the old industrial economy. In the early 1960s, when the German economic miracle had helped put the western part of the then-bifurcated country back on its feet, about 1.7 million people were employed in the mining and engineering companies in the Ruhr. Demand for coal declined after the 1960s, and the economy of this area underwent a structural transformation. Many of the old smokestack industries went into terminal decline. Newer forms of hi-tech manufacturing and services took their place.

An Indian company now owns a small part of the Ruhr economy. Carl Dan Peddinghaus (CDP) is one of the first companies to be set up in the Ruhr. It was founded in Ennepetal way back in 1839 — and was bought over in 2003 by Bharat Forge, one of India's best auto components companies. The sale of one of Germany's oldest industrial firms to an Indian firm is a testament to the way some of the best Indian companies are forging global links. They have been in the vanguard of India's rapid reintegration into the world economy over the past 15 years. The private sector's international ambitions were once satisfied with a stray licensing agreement or a small export order. Now, it is likely to be a full-fledged acquisition in another part of the world.

It has been a painful journey for many wannabe MNCs. Though they now proudly venture abroad to meet the competition, it was not so long ago that they had to be dragged kicking and screaming into a more competitive world. After all, there were memories of an easy life to be overcome. Indian companies were once content to earn fat profits behind high walls of protective tariffs (or rather, those Indian companies who were lucky or corrupt enough to bag a license from the government). So their equanimity was shattered when the economy was opened up in 1991, and Indian consumers were given more choice. The first response was a shrill cry to protect national interests. Then came a sharp recession and a long period of painful restructuring. Some good emerged from the heat of competition: the more efficient companies cut costs, sold off business lines that were either unprofitable or peripheral, and invested in enhancing productivity.

The results are now evident. Many Indian companies have gained the competitive strengths to venture out abroad to buy, sell, and acquire. A comparison between the financials of many large Indian companies over the past 10 years will tell the story in terms of stark numbers. An ever-growing number of large companies in

India are borrowing capital from the global financial markets, often bypassing the Indian financial system altogether. They are exporting and importing like never before. Some are employing global talent. Yet, these are the first tentative attempts to build Indian MNCs that stand out, because it is the most telling indication that the old sense of hopelessness that pervaded every discussion on globalization is receding very fast.

There is still a long way to go. Even today, when the top brass of an Indian company sits down to allocate capital, it is very likely that the major part of their time will be used to decide about which parts of India to invest in. Global acquisitions have often been opportunistic — something is up for sale so why do not we buy it? The fact that it is global acquisitions that have led India Inc.'s forays into the outside world partly suggests that there is less method in the madness than is commonly assumed. A large Indian company with global ambitions is still unlikely to allocate capital across borders with the same agnosticism as, say, an HSBC or a Unilever. There are still home country hang-ups.

That said, nobody in his right mind could deny that the globalization of Indian industry is one of the defining trends in modern India.

THE WORLD IS NOT ENOUGH

Why do we see the emergence of Indian MNCs? Are they any different from their peers in other parts of Asia? Let us go back for a moment to the purchase of CDP in Germany by Bharat Forge. At the time of the sale, CDP was a supplier to the likes of BMW, Volkswagen, Audi, Daimler-Chrysler, Volvo, Scania, and Ford. A presence in the world's large car manufacturing hubs helps get business, even in a world where geography is less important than before. That is what Bharat Forge sought — a manufacturing unit that almost sits in the shadow of some of Europe's largest car manufacturing plants. At one stroke, a medium-sized company situated in Pune (a city near Mumbai that straddles the industrial and services economies) got some of the world's best-known car and truck companies as clients. That one acquisition opened doors for a company that has since actively pursued the globalization agenda. Bharat Forge has made other global acquisitions after the CDP purchase.

Others in the Indian auto components industry have also actively sought out global acquisitions.

These acquisitions have been relatively quiet affairs. India's emerging multinationals have not spawned the waves of fear that the Japanese did in the 1980s or the Chinese have done in recent years when they made global acquisitions (the audacious bid by Mittal Steel to take control of Arcelor does not qualify; though Laxmi Mittal is an Indian, his firm is run out of London and has no manufacturing capacity in his home country). There have been no eye-popping deals like Sony's $3.4 billion purchase of Columbia Pictures in 1989 or the attempt by China National Oil Corporation in 2005 to buy Unocal, the ninth-largest oil company in the United States, for $18.5 billion. The acquisition of an American or European firm by an Indian firm has not yet been discussed thread-bare in the US Senate or the European Parliament; at least, not yet.

Yet companies like Bharat Forge have been building up their global businesses with calm intent. Already, consumers in the West come into contact with Indian MNCs now and then — when they step into the Pierre Hotel on New York's Fifth Avenue (which Indian Hotels took control of after signing a management contract in 2005); when they sip Tetley tea in a restaurant in London's West End (bought by Tata Tea in 2000); when they drive a Daewoo truck on a highway in Italy (bought by Tata Motors in 2004); when they watch a football match in Lisbon on a television that has a Thompson picture tube inside it (bought by Videocon in 2005); or when they paint their house using a product of Berger Paints in Singapore (bought by Asian Paints in 2002). And there have been other acquisitions that involve business assets that the man on the street does not touch and feel — oilfields in some of the nastiest spots in Africa, undersea cables that carry bandwidth across continents, or copper mines in Zambia.

Yet, despite all this hectic activity, the numbers are not very impressive. The total amount of money spent by Indian companies on their overseas acquisitions is less than $10 billion; the largest M&A deals in the rich countries cross the $10 billion mark with unfailing regularity these days. The Indian corporate sector as a whole (and over many years) has barely been able to equal the minimum benchmark that brings an M&A deal into a top-notch league table these days. So what is the fuss all about?

There are three important facts that we should consider. They give interesting clues about the nature of India's transition from protectionism to globalization. First, the recent global acquisitions by Indian companies have been done by entrepreneurial companies rather than (as in China) by state-owned giants. The only exception here is the purchase of foreign oilfields by government companies that have been asked to secure long-term fuel supplies for a growing economy. Second, Indian companies have not ventured out because of any saturation in their home markets. Quite to the contrary, in fact. For instance, there is ample scope to build more hotels or sell more televisions in India. In the 1990s the Korean *chaebol* and US retailers moved into other countries because their own home markets were running out of growth options. India's large industrial groups are displaying global ambitions *despite* attractive growth possibilities at home. Third, and most importantly, these global ambitions are proof of a new and vibrant corporate sector in the world's latest tiger economy — one that is fast shedding its fear of foreign trade and investment. In 1998, for example, many Indian companies had the cash to participate in the garage sale of corporate assets that was taking place across East Asia in the aftermath of the 1997 financial crisis. Not a single Indian company actually went into Asia and bought companies on the cheap. What was lacking was the will to venture out.

The recent burst of activity did not happen out of the blue. It is the culmination of a long process of change. India Inc.'s globalization has gone through three broad phases. The first-phase was a sort of escape from the high-security prison that the Indian economy had become in the 1970s. There were dozens of tight restrictions imposed on companies that wanted to grow. The economy was blighted by widespread shortages, yet companies were not allowed to expand capacity. A few industrial groups decided to satisfy their aspirations abroad. Aditya Birla, who was then part of the unified Birla family before it split in the early 1980s, set up Thai Rayon way back in 1974 to manufacture viscose rayon staple fiber in Thailand. He then moved into other countries like Indonesia, eventually building a global corporation that was being stymied in its home country. Gurcharan Das, formerly a senior executive with Proctor & Gamble and now a respected liberal columnist, once quoted Birla as saying:

> "We produce staple fibre in Thailand, for which we buy pulp in Canada. This fibre, made in Thailand, is sent to Indonesia for converting to yarn in our unit there. This yarn is then exported

from Indonesia to Belgium, where it is made into carpets, and finally the carpet is exported to Canada!"

Das added a pertinent observation: "We should pause and reflect that Aditya Birla was an Indian, and yet India does not figure in this global value added chain. Why? The reason is simple — our economy was closed."[2]

The second phase of globalization started in the 1980s. The economy was gradually opened up. Though import tariffs continued to be sky-high, the worst constraints on domestic expansion were removed. The government realized that it had to dump its old belief that there was no future in exports. The rupee was allowed to gradually decline in order to make Indian exports competitive. Indian companies tentatively started moving out into the world. Most of the action was restricted to either increasing exports or signing joint-venture agreements. Physical presence in foreign markets was often restricted to marketing offices in places like London, New York, and Singapore. Capital controls were still firmly in place, and companies were not allowed to use foreign currency to buy companies abroad.

The big moment of release came in 1991, when Manmohan Singh launched serious economic reforms at a time when India was just days away from defaulting on its international loans and the old guard was paralyzed with fear. Unfortunately, Indian companies myopically misread the impact of these reforms, spending many years arguing for protection from "unfair" foreign competition. In September 1993, some of the biggest names in Indian industry met at the Belvedere Club in Mumbai's Oberoi Hotel. While they were careful to speak in favor of economic reforms, they asked the government to ensure a "level-playing field." In effect, they asked for more time to get their act together before they were asked to face full-blown global competition. Thankfully, the government of the day did not succumb to all that high-powered and slightly hysterical lobbying. That meeting of India's corporate chiefs was a contemporary proof of the truth of Adam Smith's[3] famous and sardonic comment: "People of the same trade seldom meet together even for merriment and diversion, but the conversation ends in a conspiracy against the public or some contrivance to raise prices." It was the public (or consumers) who would have suffered if the Bombay Club (as it was later dubbed) had had its way.

That Indian companies were slow to understand the potential that lay hidden within them is not the whole story, however. Economic policy also played a part in the faltering advance of globalization in India. As part of the core philosophy of India's economic reforms, financial markets were liberalized more slowly than product markets. That ensured a watered-down version of globalization. So while lower tariffs helped Indian companies become more competitive and gradually link themselves to global production chains, especially in areas such as auto components and engineering, companies found it harder to acquire abroad.

The Asian crisis of 1997 made the Reserve Bank of India (RBI) even more cautious about an open capital account, since the only two major Asian countries that did not experience a run on their currencies were India and China; and both had closed capital accounts. At the same time, Indian companies did not try to take part in the garage sales of assets that were common across the crisis-hit region in 1998. They were too busy adjusting to the needs of an open economy to focus their minds on foreign acquisitions. Indian companies and regulators became even more cautious after the spectacular meltdown in Asia in 1997. There was more circumspection about foreign investment than there was about foreign trade. It was not until the year 2000, when the economy was on more stable ground and foreign exchange reserves were comfortable, that the government and the central bank felt confident enough to encourage India's wannabe MNCs to venture out. And venture out they did.

THE NEW ECONOMICS OF TRADE

One of the most interesting features of public debate today is the comparison between the current round of globalization and the previous one in the late 19th and early 20th centuries. There are many points of difference between these two epochs. A lot has been written about the quantity of trade (as expressed by the trade-to-GDP ratios) in Globalization Ver 1.0 and Globalization Ver 2.0. The growing importance of services in international trade is also a well-documented fact. The torrent of short-term capital splashing across national boundaries today would not be known to a Victorian financier in 19th-century London. However, the qualitative change in world trade is equally important, though curiously ignored. One of the most significant facets of Globalization Ver 2.0 is the growing importance of global supply chains. This has implications for both companies and policy makers.

The modern production structure in many industries is like a jigsaw puzzle. Each country adds its own little piece. So very often there is buying and selling of these little pieces across international borders, rather than the entire jigsaw puzzle itself. Or, in other words, trade is often in intermediates rather than in finished products. A company like Dell Computers epitomizes the new production structure of the world economy. It is a core building block of its business model. Dell does not manufacture its own components or subassemblies. It sources everything from semiconductors to keyboards from an intricate supply chain that crisscrosses America, Europe, and Asia.

There are other examples. Ford's cars have parts produced in 14 countries and are assembled in nine countries. Or look at the Barbie Doll, which little girls from San Francisco to Shanghai bully their parents into buying. The plastic and hair for the doll are obtained from Taiwan and Japan. The doll is assembled in Indonesia, China, and Malaysia. The moulds come from the United States, as do the paints used to decorate the dolls. China also supplies the cotton cloth used for their clothes.

Many economists have commented on the trend toward distributed production and assembly, though they have not had enough success in measuring it. "The rising integration of world markets has brought with it a disintegration of the production process," writes University of California economist Robert C. Feenstra in a 1998 article.[4] Paul Krugman has called it the slicing of the value chain. Critics often point out that it is only the low-value bit of the production chain that is sent to countries with cheap labor. Wages thus get depressed in the West while Asian labor is forced to work in sweatshops. This common criticism does not take into account three factors. First, for a young Asian, a job with a supplier to Nike or Reebok is often nothing short of deliverance from a life of extreme poverty. Second, countries can gradually move up the value chain as they gain the requisite skills, as South Korea and Taiwan have done. Third, in its effect on the wages of unskilled labor in the West, such outsourcing is no different from technological innovation that substitutes labor with capital. Why should one be acceptable and the other unacceptable?

Many countries in Asia have benefited by engaging in such production chains. India, despite its recent enthusiastic attempts, has been only a modest participant in this new production structure. And that has been a substantial failing, because one of India's big challenges is to provide jobs to millions of unskilled workers. Precision manufacturing using skilled labor or jobs for software engineers are not enough to launch a frontal attack on unemployment. In fact, being part of a global supply chain has benefits that are far greater than is commonly understood.

> "Estimates show that the benefits of trade liberalization that are accompanied by the establishment of international supply chain arrangements between firms in the industrial and less developed countries is between *10 to 20 times higher* than those accruing from trade liberalization alone"[5] (italics added).

When the returns that accrue to a country that actively participates in global supply chains are so large, it is easier to counter the specious claims advanced by the defenders of protectionism when they set out to show why foreign capital is not important (if not outright dangerous). These honorable people often dismiss the need for foreign capital by arguing that it can only be a minor component in a nation's total capital formation. That is an inadequate way of looking at Foreign Direct Investment (FDI). It is well established that FDI helps transfer skills, knowledge, and organizational capabilities from one country to another.

Similarly, being part of a global supply chain has two important advantages that are often absent from public debates, at least in India. First, the fine slicing of the production chain allows countries to focus on those parts of the process where they are competitive. India has lagged behind the rest of Asia in the manufacture of digital hardware. But it now occupies an important position in one part of the hardware chain — research and development. India hosts the labs of companies such as Intel, Microsoft, and Motorola. In automobiles, Sundaram Fasteners has been supplying millions of radiator caps to General Motors. It is the same story in textiles, where Indian firms are doing well in some parts of the manufacturing process. There is a public policy lesson here that Indian mandarins would do well to learn. Companies can build competitive advantage in certain functions, and not necessarily in an entire industry.

Second, global supply chains work on a very subtle flow of inventory and information. The ruling mantra is "Just in Time" (JIT). Suppliers have to send their material at almost the precise moment their client wants it. A mountain of inventory is a crime. None of this will be possible if transport and communication infrastructure is of poor quality. One of the biggest failings of Indian exporters is their inability to meet supply schedules. They are often caught in a logjam along the national highways and at the ports. The very fact of being part of a global supply chain forces countries to upgrade their transport and communication infrastructure. It is perhaps not a coincidence that the three areas where there have been noticeable improvements in infrastructure in India have been telecom, roads, and ports. Each helps move inventory and information around. Other sectors like power and water have lagged behind.

While the contribution of FDI to overall capital formation was very low in countries such as Korea and Taiwan, the contribution to exports and employment is very high. It is much the same with China. Large parts of its exports originate from MNC subsidiaries or local companies that supply to MNCs. As I have been writing this book, one of the biggest policy debates in India has been whether FDI should be allowed in retailing. There were genuine fears that the entry of the likes of Wal-Mart would destroy millions of small shopkeepers in India. Yet, cooler heads argued that there would be advantages as well.

> "Over a decade ago, we did some far-reaching things that put the sparkle back in the eyes of our educated urban youngsters. What right do we have to deny to the millions of kids growing up today the same opportunity in our fields, factories and stores? The only way not to let them down is to create supply chains that will connect our farms and factories to the consumers of the world. For that we need 100 per cent foreign direct investment in the Indian retail sector. There is not a moment to lose" (Infosys Technologies CEO Nandan Nilekani in a perceptive column in *The Indian Express*).[6]

In a way, Nilekani argued, a modern retail chain acts like a pipe that connects producers and consumers. Plugging into this pipe will allow millions of Indians to benefit from globalization.

> "A friend from Fortune magazine once told me that what the submarine cable is to India (a gigantic pipe to ship knowledge services to the West), Wal-Mart is to China (a gigantic pipe to ship manufactured products to the West)!"

The new structure of production demands fresh thinking by India's mandarins. No doubt they have shed their old suspicion of foreign trade that dominated policy between 1950s and 1970s. Nor do they believe in the mercantilism of the 1980s — when exports were encouraged, but imports were frowned upon. Most of the people who matter in government now realize that imports and exports are often two sides of the same coin. A company cannot sell in the global market at competitive rates unless it can source inputs at the lowest rates possible. But now a third leap of faith is needed — a recognition that export growth is dependent on FDI as well as participation in global supply chains. To open up to trade and remain suspicious of foreign investment is an odd and eventually self-defeating combination.

THE GLOBAL INDIAN ECONOMY

It is not surprising that a country that has suffered colonial rule over two centuries has a deep suspicion of foreign trade and investment. After all, it was the East India Company rather than the British Crown that first stripped India of its political independence. Yet, other countries with colonial memories have taken advantage of the current round of globalization, which is being sustained by multilateral negotiations rather than gunboat diplomacy. India has been too slow to embrace the biggest opportunity of our times, because it is still caught in an ideological time warp.

One of my favorite anecdotes on economic policy has been told by Robert Rubin in his autobiography, *In An Uncertain World*. It tells us a lot about how sometimes even a very able politician has to be convinced about the advantages of trade.

> "Protecting industries is usually appealing, because the negative consequences of free trade are so visible.... In a discussion with President Clinton ... I mentioned that one sector where we needed to push for reduced trade barriers was fish. Clinton remembered ... seeing some poor fisherman casting their lines....

He wasn't going to do anything to hurt those vulnerable people. 'But Mr. President,' I said, 'to help those poor fishermen, you're going to prevent the vastly greater benefit that would come to the poor ... from being able to buy cheap fish'"[7] (*Clinton saw the point in no time*).

While the rapid globalization of India's corporate sector is a positive development, the plain fact is that the Indian economy as a whole has a long way to go before it is fully integrated with the rest of the world. Every year, *Foreign Policy* magazine and consulting firm A.T. Kearney publish a ranking of countries based on the extent of their globalization. This includes not just trade and investment, but also parameters such as travel, technological connectivity, and political engagement. India regularly finds itself at the bottom of the pile. In 2005, it was 61st out of a list of 62 countries. Only Iran was less globalized than India. Even countries like Kenya, Bangladesh, and Egypt were ahead. China was at 54, but it is advancing rapidly up the charts.[8]

A lot will follow if trade and investment across India's borders increase rapidly. India spent far too many years in a shell, oblivious of what was happening elsewhere. Remember that India accounted for 7% of world trade in the 1890s. It was an active participant in the first wave of globalization that crested before the guns went off in Europe in 1914. Most countries went into a protectionist shell over the subsequent four decades, and paid a heavy price in terms of low economic growth. Global trade surged once again after the end of the Second World War. India remained a mute spectator. Its share of global trade had fallen precipitously — to 0.4% by 1990. Japan's went up from 0.4% in 1950 to over 10% in 1993. These were journeys in opposite directions, and the economic record tells us which was the smarter choice. Many Asian countries grew on the back of buoyant exports after the 1950s. India stagnated.

A core belief in India's early development strategy was that the rest of the world was not to be trusted. A fear of international trade and investment is not completely unfounded in a country that was under the colonial yoke for nearly two centuries. Many of the leaders who led India to independence viewed foreign trade as a "whirlpool of economic imperialism." As a result, by 1980, India's foreign trade was a mere 16.6% of its GDP. Forget active trading nations like South Korea (75.5%) or

Thailand (54.4%). Even prereform China had a higher trade-to-GDP ratio (22.3%). It means that even communist China — at a time when it was catching its breath after the madness of its Maoist era and just around the time that Deng introduced his market reforms — was less suspicious of foreign trade than socialist India was.

There were many strands in this policy of extreme autarky. The rupee was overvalued. The government wanted to import capital goods to pursue its development strategy, and a strong rupee helped keep the costs of these inputs down. At the same time, exchange controls, high tariffs, and import quotas deprived consumers and private companies of the benefit from cheap imports. When the large-scale import of capital goods led India into a balance of payments crisis as early as 1957, the import controls were tightened. The sensible way out would have been to let the rupee slide, cut taxes on imports and be more enthusiastic about exports. This was not done till as late as the 1980s.

Though India has been slowly opening its doors to the world, it still leads a relatively hermetic existence. As always, a comparison with an enthusiastic trading nation like China tells us a lot. Foreign trade is about a third of India's GDP; at 46%, China is far ahead. China's share of world exports climbed from 1.9% in 1989 to 6% in 2003. That is the one big reason why India fails to make as much of an impact on the world as China does. In the years 2003 and 2004, India accounted for about a fifth of Asian growth and a tenth of world growth. That seems impressive — till you look at China. Then India pales in comparison. China accounted for 53% of Asian growth and 28% of world growth. Naturally, India is seen as neither a threat nor a blessing by other economies. China's relentless export machine strikes a chord of fear in foreign capitals. Meanwhile, its gluttonous appetite for imports has lifted the fortunes of many — from Japan's engineering companies to Brazil's soyabean farmers to Saudi Arabia's oil sheikhs. China's growing impact on the world economy allows it not just to exercise economic power. It also gives it more foreign policy clout — something that India's policy establishment has belatedly realized. Foreign trade gives a country more power to hammer diplomatic deals.

Yet, there is little doubt that India is well on its way to becoming more deeply involved in the global economy (and hence global politics as well). The International Monetary Fund (IMF) estimates that between 2004 and 2010, Indian exports will more than double and imports will triple. Foreign trade has been growing faster than the economy as a whole for several years now. The government too has been assiduously cutting import tariffs since 1991. Though the average tariff rate of 28.3% in 2004 was still far higher than what it was in most other Asian economies, it still was a great improvement over the 79%-plus rate of protection Indian industry had before 1991. Also, given the slow pace of progress in the various multilateral trade forums in recent years, the Indian government has been busy signing preferential trade agreements with neighbors such as Thailand and Sri Lanka. These policies should help India integrate faster with the rest of the world (Table 6).

Table 6
Simple Mean Tariff (on all products)

	1990	2004
India	79.0	28.3
China	40.4	9.8

Source: World Development Indicators 2005.

India is already feeling the effects of its second coming into the global economy. Let us take a look at the pattern of corporate investments, for example. India experienced an investment boom in the mid-1990s, as industry went into raptures after the introduction of liberal economic reforms. This boom petered out soon after, leaving behind a trail of unviable projects and bad loans. Looking back, it is evident that the few investments were based on global competitiveness. So projects faltered after protection levels were brought down through the 1990s. Meanwhile, the RBI too pushed up interest rates to calm the euphoria. A severe industrial slowdown followed. After that, Indian companies restricted investments into areas where there were no direct threats from imports. Telecom is an obvious example. It was lavished with billions of dollars of investments (both domestic and foreign), despite an investment drought elsewhere in the economy. Other non-tradable sectors such as insurance, financial services, and road building also attracted money.

The two exceptions to this were auto manufacturing (which continues to be protected by high tariffs) and software services (where India was competitive from day one). Corporate investments revived in 2005. The current round of investments is different from the one in the mid-1990s in one subtle yet significant way. Companies poured money into new factories in 1994 and 1995 because they were attracted by the promise of a liberalized India. Ten years later, the attraction is of a globalized India. So a lot of money is flowing into sectors where Indian companies have achieved global competitiveness. Pharmaceuticals, textiles, and steel are obvious examples. Indian manufacturers in these areas are getting coupled with global supply chains.

Being part of a global supply chain is a great way to increase trade. India is yet to fully participate in the regional supply chains that have been strung across Asia and drive a lot of the inter-regional trade in this part of the world. India accounts for just 1% of the trade between Asian countries. A lot of this is linked to investment. One reason why China is so big in exports is that it attracts lots of foreign investment. This is where India has failed.

Yet, India looks likely to keep on globalizing. Says the IMF:

"A dynamic and open Indian economy would have an important impact on the world economy. If India continues to embrace globalisation and reform, Indian imports could increasingly operate as a driver of global growth as it is one of a handful of economies forecast to have a growing working-age population over the next 40 years."[9]

NOTES

1. "My Ranbaxy Experience", by D.S. Brar, *Business World*, June 7, 2004.
2. "Swades and Aditya Birla", by Gurcharan Das, *Times of India*, August 18, 1998.
3. Adam Smith, An Inquiry Into The Nature And Cause of The Wealth of Nations, edited by Edwin Cannan, *The Modern Library*, 1937, p.128.
4. "Integration of Trade and Disintegration of Production In The Global Economy", Robert C. Feenastra, *Journal of Economic Perspectives*, Autumn 1998.
5. Asian Development Outlook 2003, Asian Development Bank, the chapter on global value chains is available at: http://www.adb.org/Documents/Books/ADO/2003/part3_3-5.asp#p3-5d.
6. "Retail FDI: Just Do It", by Nandan Nilekani, *Indian Express*, September 2, 2005.
7. In An Uncertain World, by Robert E. Rubin, *Random House*, 2003.
8. Available at: http://www.atkearny.com.
9. World Economic Outlook, September 2005, IMF (2005), the box on this issue is available at: http://www.imf.org/Pubs/FT/weo/2005/02/pdf/chapter1.pdf.

Chapter 6

The Financial
Revolution

CREDIT, WHERE IT IS DUE

Indians have started saving more than ever before. The savings rate was around 24% of GDP through most of the 1990s. It is now just short of 30% of GDP. Household savings are going up because of higher incomes and changing demographics. Corporate savings have been steady. And public sector savings too have been showing early signs of improvement ever since government finances started gradually improving in 2004. All this means that the pool from which companies, traders, and farmers can draw capital to finance growth is that much bigger. The rise in the Indian savings and investment rates has been one of the most underrated economic trends of our times.

It will be the job of the financial sector to ensure that the higher savings are used productively. While the capital market, venture capital funds, and specialist financial institutions do have an important role to play here, it is the banks that have to bear the main burden. That is because India's financial system is still dominated by banks. The banks will have to meet two challenges. One, efficiency: money raised from depositors has to be used to profitably fund the right sectors and projects. Two, financial depth: banks will have to reach out to as many Indians as possible. Why? Because financial development is closely linked to economic development and bank credit-to-GDP ratios tend to move in step with average incomes.[1]

The Indian financial system has had a mixed record on the question of meeting these two goals simultaneously. India's banks have struggled to maintain a balance between financial health and financial depth, often veering more to one side than the other. There have been times when banks have reached out to newer customers and geographical areas, but these bursts of expansion have often left them nursing huge balance sheet wounds in the form of bad loans. There have also been times when the financial parameters of banks have improved remarkably, though these journeys back to financial health have often been made possible by a flight from risk-taking and credit growth.

This seesawing has partly been the result of the regulatory environment. The men and women who control the flow of money and credit in any economy have to balance the twin goals of maintaining financial stability and fostering financial innovation. Leaning too much on one side is fraught with danger. The Reserve Bank of India (RBI) has done a stellar job in recent years in keeping the financial system on an even keel. The Indian financial system has never really succumbed to the waves of panic that have dislocated so many economies in Asia and Latin America since the Bretton Woods system fell apart in 1971. The problem is that the quest for financial stability has smothered financial innovation. Indian banks have preferred to play safe, especially since banking reforms were initiated in 1993. One unfortunate fallout of the preference for stability over innovation is that banks have not tried to reach out to the urban and rural poor — the very people who need money from the financial system so that they can generate wealth and participate more actively in India's striking economic transformation.

This is now changing. The financial health of Indian banks is now better than it has ever been in the past few decades. At the same time, their customer base has changed remarkably. Large companies no longer depend very heavily on banks for funds. There are two reasons for this. First, the better companies have learned to work with tighter inventories, shorter working capital cycles, and their own cash. Second, easier access to the financial markets (including global equity and bond markets) has allowed large Indian companies to raise money directly from investors at rates that are often lower than what the traditional banker offered them. They have been quite happy to bypass the banking system.

So banks are looking at new avenues to deploy their money. Consumer credit and mortgage finance have grown at explosive rates since the late 1990s. The readiness to fund the ambitions of the middle-class is the best indicator that banks are eyeing the ordinary Indian. Lending to small companies too has grown rapidly. The big challenge now is to see how much lower banks can move down the income pyramid — all the way down to the rural poor — without denting their profitably. I shall return to this a little later.

In general, while the Indian banking sector has done a far better job than many of its regional peers on the efficiency and stability fronts, it has been a bit of a laggard in creating financial depth. The challenge in the years ahead is to address the latter problem without sacrificing financial efficiency and stability.

THE CASE OF THE TAXI COMPANY

First, let us take a look at the strength of the Indian banking system and the wisdom of the regulators who forced banks to clean up their balance sheets, especially in the 1990s. A comparison with other parts of Asia is instructive.

I had a visitor to my office in the early months of 1997. He worked for Peregrine, a high-flying Hong Kong financial company then known for its raw aggression. This gentleman was soon lecturing me with abandon about how India's timid financial policies would be its undoing. He merrily rattled off what he thought was one failure after another — from the refusal to mop up short-term dollars from eager global investors to the tight control on bank investments in areas such as equity and real estate. Look at Thailand. Look at Indonesia, he kept telling me.

A few months later, financial systems across East and South-East Asia tumbled like a set of dominoes. Part of the problem was that many Asian companies had piles of short-term dollar debt and many banks in the region had made large investments in equity and real estate. They were like little bombs hidden in the books of Asian banks. When they went off, bank balance sheets were in tatters. Investors panicked even more and pulled out their short-term loans from the region, sending several economies into a downward spiral. Meanwhile, banks were paralyzed because equity prices tumbled and most of the real estate projects they had carelessly funded, faltered.

I read with some amusement that one of the banks that went into bankruptcy during these manic months was Peregrine. It had lent $270 million to Steady Safe, a taxi company in Indonesia that had links to the Suharto family. Steady Safe's turnover was all of

$9 million when it took its loan from Peregrine. India's caution in opening up its capital account and its banking sector has paid off. Even the worst cases of bad lending in India (and there have been many) never came close to the ridiculous decisions that one heard about from the rest of Asia, like Peregrine's $270 million loan to a tiny taxi company in Jakarta.

FINANCIAL SECTOR REFORM: THE DEBATE

Peregrine's investment in that taxi company was just a small indication of a far bigger problem of macroeconomic management. Eventually, financial systems across East and South-East Asia imploded in the second half of 1997. It all began in Thailand that July. And then, in a few manic months, the others followed. Indonesia, Malaysia and South Korea — the crisis spread with ruthless efficiency.

Banks all over the region tumbled in the wake of an unprecedented financial tsunami. Could India hold back the waves of panic that were lashing the rest of Asia? There were a hundred dark rumors in the air. Around the same time, one prestigious European brokerage firm had published a research report that dripped with pessimism. It said that the Indian banking system too was walking on water. It would soon drown in a sea of bad loans. And that the official claim that Indian banks were safe should not be believed.

A few weeks later, when the report was still being circulated surreptitiously like some underground manifesto, I met a senior RBI official at its headquarters in Mumbai. Was the dark underside of Indian banking being hidden from public view by a thick fog of accounting? "I think the central bank knows more than some smart set of equity analysts," he said bitterly. "Just wait and see."

He was right. India was untouched. Asia's financial crisis did subside, but it left behind shattered economies and human suffering. The one big lesson that the world's policy elite learnt after 1997 and 1998 was that you cannot have a strong economy without a strong banking system. India, which had been under immense pressure to open up its banking sector and capital account in the years leading to the 1997 crisis, saw its caution being vindicated. The only two major countries in developing Asia to escape the selling fury that toppled other currencies and economies were India and China; both had closed capital accounts and tightly controlled banking systems.

The countries that had been worst-hit by the financial crisis of 1997 had allowed their companies and banks to go on a borrowing spree, even if what they brought home was often large quantities of short-term dollars that had been raised at low interest rates but that could flee at a moment's notice (which they eventually did). The central banks in the region were committed to protecting a fixed exchange rate between their currencies and the dollar; so, in effect, the risk of a currency shock was being borne by the government rather than by the borrowers. A lot of this money was used to fund investments in the stock market and real estate.

The RBI had a different approach, one that seemed too timid to the hordes of global financiers coming into India in those years. The RBI did not make a fetish of any particular exchange rate; all it has bothered about is excess volatility in the foreign exchange market. There have been times when the RBI has moved away from its own core principle, as when it intervened in the foreign exchange market with furious intent in the early years of this decade to prevent the rupee from appreciating against the dollar. But in general, by being flexible about exchange rates, India's central bank ensured that it is the borrowers who bear the risk of currency movements. That, in itself, was a disincentive for wild borrowing.

There are other elements in India's financial management strategy that are now lauded. While the current account — which covers regular trade in goods and services — was made convertible in the early years of reform, there has been far more circumspection when it comes to opening up the capital account. The official policy has been that premature capital account convertibility is to be avoided. In the early months of 1997, before the crisis struck Asia, a committee headed by former RBI deputy governor S.S. Tarapore put down certain preconditions that had to be met before the rupee became truly convertible: for example, a low fiscal deficit, a stronger banking system, ample foreign exchange reserves, and a mandated inflation target.

The severity of the damage in Asia set the clock back. Convertibility was put on hold. But the RBI did gradually open up the capital account after a few years. Today, Indian companies have immense freedom to go abroad to borrow and acquire. Multinationals have no problems bringing in and taking out capital. Equity flows into the stock market, too, are unhindered by any special regulations against foreigners. At the time this book was being written, the two significant areas where capital controls remained were the bond markets (where there are caps on the amount of foreign investment in domestic bonds) and foreign investments by individuals (where Indian citizens are not allowed to invest more than $25,000 a year abroad). So India already has large dollops of capital account convertibility. And there are clear signs that the government wants to move to full convertibility by the end of the decade.

However, the caution with which India has handled its financial sector has been a double-edged sword. While it ensured that the Indian economy was unharmed in 1997, it also helped make a fetish of financial stability, which is valued above everything else in India. There will continue to be debates about whether India has been too slow in opening up its capital account. What matters is the record. According to the World Bank, there have been 113 banking crises in 93 countries between 1975 and 1999 (a full-blown banking crisis occurs when most of the banking capital in a country is wiped out). Economists have studied the issue of financial stability in detail only after the 1970s, when the old Bretton Woods system unraveled. The first lot of researchers trained their attentions on the effect of loose monetary and fiscal policies on financial stability. Research then started focusing on the nature of herd behavior in the currency markets and of self-fulfilling expectations. But it was only after the Asian crisis of 1997 that economists started looking at the link between banking and currency crises — the so-called twin crises. In a paper written in 1999, Graciela Kaminsky and Carmen Reinhart say: "Many countries that have had currency crises have also had full-fledged domestic banking crises around the same time."[2]

India has had just one major financial crisis: in 1990–1991, when the current account deficit widened in the wake of the first Gulf War but could not be financed as investors pulled money out of India. Otherwise, the central bank has not allowed enthusiasm to run ahead of reality. The Asian crisis of 1997 too was also a sobering episode for the Indian financial establishment. But it is another event — way back in 1969 — that has borne the deepest imprint on the Indian financial system.

THE DEFINING MOMENT

The most important and controversial decision in India's financial history is that taken by the government in July 1969 to nationalize the country's top banks. A lot of the banking achievements and failures since then can be traced to this defining moment. It is widely believed that the radical economic reforms of 1991 — which finally lifted the thick blanket of controls that had suffocated Indian enterprise for several decades — were the most important economic events in modern Indian history. The official historians of the RBI differ with the popular consensus. According to them, the honor should go to the controversial decision taken in July 1969 to nationalize India's 14 largest commercial banks. "By any measure," they write in the third volume of the central bank's official history

> "this was the defining economic event of not just the 1960s but the next three decades. Its reverberations have still not died down. It remains, without doubt, the single most important economic decision taken by any government since 1947. Not even the reforms of 1991 are comparable in their consequences — political, social and, of course, economic."[3]

Whether the nationalization of banks was actually a more significant decision than the 1991 reforms is a matter of debate. What is indisputable is that bank nationalization is comparable with the reforms of 1991 in terms of its long-term significance. They are an odd couple in many ways: bank nationalization dramatically extended the power of the government over the economy while economic reforms led to a sharp curtailment of these powers. But there is a common strand running through both in the sense that they both tried to empower common people: bank nationalization helped the man on the street get access to commercial credit while the reforms of 1991 empowered consumers through competition and free markets.

Access to the modern financial system is still very limited in India, and is one of the most important drawbacks of the prevailing economic structure. It was even worse 40 years ago. This was the reason why the government took over banks in the first place. It was argued that nationalization was the only way to deepen the financial system, spread the credit culture and bring more people into the circle of development. Did it do all this? We shall examine the record presently.

IS THE BANKING SYSTEM LIKE A RARE MING VASE?

The numbers tell the story in very stark terms. The total number of bank deposit accounts in India is a mere 60% of the total population. Many Indians undoubtedly have multiple banks accounts. This means that perhaps one out of every two Indians does not have a bank account. In some of the poorer regions of the country — like the state of Bihar — nearly two out of three residents do not have a bank account. If one considers a bank account as something like a passport to the modern economy — a basic document — then the paucity of bank accounts means that large numbers of Indians are not in a position to participate in the modern economy.

Many of those outside the banking system are extremely poor or live in remote areas, so there is a question about how banks can offer them deposit products without running up losses. The ability to offer small deposit and loan products to the poor, and that too as a profitable business rather than as part of some wishy-washy corporate social responsibility scheme, will severely test the innovativeness of Indian banks. It will entail adopting new technologies, new marketing strategies, new products, new risk management strategies, as well as forging alliances with local civic groups.

Forget the poor for a moment. Indian banks have often shied away from lending to companies as well in recent years — an indication of how quickly they can withdraw into their shells. These episodes of banking inertia tell us a lot about how worrisome the problem really is. Through most of the decade after 1996, banks were happy using large parts of the money they raised from the public (about 40%) to fund the government's deficit. Buying government bonds is an easy game — there is no risk of default. In fact, banks have made a lot of money in recent years from their bond portfolios, as interest rates fell and bond prices rose. The Indian government's huge fiscal deficit and the eagerness of the banks to fund it has, in effect, denied credit to millions of farmers, traders, and small businessmen.

The point is that fleeing from risk-taking can harm an economy. While the grand debates on the future of modern financial systems — like capital adequacy, consolidation, risk management, and technology — are eagerly fought in India, the sad fact that a large section of Indians is still outside the ambit of a modern financial system is often glossed over. Every financial system is fragile and needs to be handled with great care. But it cannot be treated like a rare Ming vase that only a privileged few are allowed to touch. That, unfortunately, is how things often happen in India.

THE TRUTH ABOUT INDIAN BANKS

The success of a financial system can be judged on two parameters. One, how stable and profitable is it? Two, how many people does it reach out to? As always, a look at the situation in Asia's two emerging economic giants is instructive. In many ways, the Indian and Chinese financial systems are mirror images of each other as far as the two key parameters (stability and reach) go. One is stable and profitable. The other is on less firm ground but has a wider reach. I remember how the movers and shakers of Mumbai's financial community had nodded their heads sagely when Prime Minister Manmohan Singh told them in the course of a speech he gave in June 2005 to commemorate the State Bank of India's 200th year: "If there is one aspect in which we can confidently assert that India is ahead of China, it is in the robustness and soundness of our banking system."[4] This is no doubt a comforting claim that has been made very often. But how justified is it?

The official data on Chinese banks is sketchy, as is so often the case. But most independent analysts believe that Chinese banks have a staggering bad loan problem. The estimates vary, ranging from 30% to 50% of the total loans. So, even if we go by the lower estimate, a third of all the money lent out by China's banks has been frittered away. In 2004, China spent a mind-blowing $45 billion to recapitalize its two largest banks, Bank of China and China Construction Bank. This throws light on two facts. One, China's banks are in a mess. Two, the government is busy cleaning up the dirt. In contrast, the latest data shows that the net Non-Performing Loans (NPLs) of the entire Indian banking sector are less than 3% of total loans. They were close to 15% a decade ago. Indian banks have sensibly used the windfall they made in bond trading in recent years to clean up their balance sheets.

End of story? No. Indian banks have undoubtedly become more efficient in the past decade. They are far less likely to pour the nation's modest savings into unviable projects. But — and this is a very important but — Indian banks have lagged behind the Chinese as far as deepening the financial system goes. They have failed to garner enough deposits and hence failed to provide enough loans to farmers, companies, and traders. India's bank credit-to-GDP ratio is about 37%, far lower than most other emerging markets where the ratio is close to 100%.

A recent study by the McKinsey Global Institute (MGI) on global financial stock (the aggregate value of bank deposits, equities, and shares in the world) makes a similar point. India's financial depth (which MGI calculates as financial stock as a percent of GDP) is 137%. China's is 323%. In other words, China's financial depth is two and a half times India's. "The bottom line is that India has far less money circulating in the financial system than one would expect, given the size of its economy," say Diana Farrell and Aneta Marcheva Key in an article in *The McKinsey Quarterly*.[5]

Why is there a lot less money circulating in the Indian financial system? This can be partly explained by the fact that China's savings rate is twice that of India. The Chinese save more and hence deposit more money into their bank accounts. But that is not the entire story. Indian banks have failed to extend their services to the poor. So it would be good to modify the terms of the popular comparison between the financial systems of India and China. India has the stronger system while China has the bigger one. This will definitely change in the years ahead. India's savings rate has started climbing. It touched an all-time high of 28.1% in 2004. This should mean that more money starts flowing into the banking system. The central bank is concerned about the lack of adequate financial inclusion. A few banks are, of their own volition and driven by commercial considerations,

Table 7
Financial Depth

| | Domestic credit provided by the banking sector (as percent of GDP) | |
	1990	2003
China	90	177.9
India	51.5	57.3
Indonesia	45.5	55.7
Japan	260.7	157.3
Malaysia	75.7	152.1
Philippines	26.9	59.5
Mexico	36.3	38.5
South Africa	97.8	158.2

Source: World Development Indicators 2005.

trying to provide banking services to the hitherto unbanked masses. Meanwhile, China too will close the efficiency lead that India has over it. China is serious about its weak banking system. India will have to become more serious about its narrow banking system. To me, that is the key issue. How does India balance the twin quests for financial stability and financial depth? (Table 7).

WAS BANK NATIONALIZATION ACTUALLY A SUCCESS?

India had faced the problem of inadequate access to finance before. In the 1950s and 1960s, economists often commented on the fact that most Indians did not have access to bank finance. They often depended on interest-free family loans or mortgaged their land and gold to local moneylenders. Interest rates for informal finance were sky-high. Workers often borrowed without any collateral. In Mumbai's working-class districts, the burly Pathans from Afghanistan who hovered at the factory gates on payday to collect their dues were objects of popular fear.

What was to be done? Such was the mood of the times that the government thought it could tackle the problem with good intentions and the enlightened judgment of its bureaucrats. There was an initial attempt in 1967 to impose "social control" on banks. That is, banks were directed to lend on a priority basis to sectors that the government thought needed money. The project did not succeed. So, in July 1969, the government took over the country's 14 largest banks. The justification was that key sectors of the economy were being denied access to credit. In a recent research paper, economists Sumon Bhoumik and Jenifer Piesse say that between 1951 and 1968, "The proportion of credit going to industry and trade increased from an already high 83% to 90%. This increase was at the cost of some crucial segments of the economy like agriculture and the small-scale sector."[6] The latter were being starved of credit by a banking system that was allergic to risk.

Bank nationalization has been demonized for a number of valid reasons. The public sector gradually became a source of patronage and loot. Nationalized banks were no exception. In fact, they were highly prized sources of power in an economy suffocating under controls. They became centers of what the US call pork barrel politics. In an era where private capital flows between nations were a mere trickle, private businesses could not borrow abroad. They had to depend on the local savings pool to fund their activities.

The equity and debt markets were small in India, so this meant that bank loans were the only oasis of capital in a barren financial system. Control over banks meant control over the economy.

LOANS CARNIVALS AND OTHER ABSURDITIES

Corrupt politicians controlled banks after 1969 — they thus had the economy by the jugular. They used their power to dish out patronage. Money was often lent out to favored interest groups, and this directly contributed to a huge bad loan problem in later decades. Finance ministers imperiously asked banks to lend to those whose support they were seeking. When the favored lenders could not repay the loans, banks were asked to let them off the hook. The discipline of price-based lending was deliberately buried. Commercial considerations were given short shrift. Capital was misallocated.

There was always a standard answer to these criticisms: this is being done for the benefit of the poor. The most astonishing attempts to buy patronage and to make banks lend without regard to any commercial considerations were the infamous loan *melas*, or loan fairs. They were the idea of Janardhana Poojary, minister of state for finance in the central government between 1982 and 1984. He was close to the then prime minister, Indira Gandhi. Poojary believed that one way to renew the moribund rural economy — and garner votes — was to force banks to lend money to villagers. So this is how the typical loan *mela* worked. The local bankers in a village would be rounded up and told to open their lending books to all comers. Then the local populace was informed that there would be a loan *mela*. The locals had to come to the bank and sign a piece of paper. If they were illiterate, then a thumbprint would do. The lucky folk could then walk away with up to Rs. 50,000, which was not an insignificant sum in those days. And no questions were asked.

All this resembled a type of deficit financing. Money was pumped into the economy. There were some immediate gains to the local economy, as the people who had taken such loans spent that largesse. But there was long-term damage done to the banks and their ability to lend to enterprises that really deserved money. Naturally, the loan *melas* were misused. Local elites used their power to grab as much as they could. They forced their loyal retainers to sign on the dotted line and took the money for themselves. Some were smart enough to take loans in the names of their cattle. Dead relatives magically came to life for one day, collected their money, and went back to where they came from. It was a season for loot. Eventually, the *melas* stopped. But the damage had been done; banks were left nursing huge bad debts.

Loan *melas* were some of the darkest moments in recent banking history in India. Although every policy was not so thoughtless, the loan *melas* give us some sense of what happened after banks were nationalized and politicians took charge. And it was not only rural landlords who walked away with pots of money. Some of India's most influential business groups too sucked banks dry. Most bankers did not bother to protest, because they would anyway be transferred to another place and another branch in a few years. So why take the trouble? But it is said that crackers were burst and sweets were distributed outside some bank branches the day Poojary finally left the finance ministry.

AN UPRIGHT MAN

The loan *melas* were clearly the most absurd manifestations of what was ostensibly social banking. They were loud affairs that advertized their absurdity. But there was a parallel process of slow degeneration. R.K. Talwar, chairman of the giant State Bank of India and one of India's ablest and most respected bankers, resigned in disgust as early as 1976 (seven years after bank nation-alization) to protest against the politicization of banking. Talwar was an incredibly visionary banker. He became the chairman of the India's biggest bank at the relatively young age of 47. As a trainee in the old Imperial Bank of India in the 1940s, Talwar had seen how the bank gave loans to companies based on their reputation rather than their financials. As State Bank of India chairman, he insisted that large companies be given loans only after their financials were examined and analyzed. At the same time, he pioneered loans to small entrepreneurs and opened bank branches in remote areas. Talwar led the way in lending to small businessmen, roadside entrepreneurs (and even reformed convicts) in a bid to give ordinary people access to capital. But when he was being pressured by the government to give a fresh loan to a defaulter who happened to have political connections, he resigned.

That a corrupt political class was able to push out an upright and outstanding banker like Talwar was an undoubted tragedy. Yet, despite all these obvious horrors, bank nationalization was successful in what it set out to do. More and more Indians were brought within the modern financial system. An awesome 58,000 new bank branches were opened in the three and a half decades after banks were nationalized. The average population covered by a bank branch has dropped from 64,000 to 16,000 from 1969 to 2005. With the availability of banking services, Indians started putting a greater proportion of their savings into bank deposits rather than physical assets. The credit culture grew. Farmers, traders, and small businessmen now have access to capital. Bank nationalization did deliver what it set out to do, though this came at the cost of financial stability. Loans grew; but so did bad loans.

AN EPISODE OF LAZY BANKING

The pendulum swung back in the 1990s and the early part of this decade. One of the key goals of the early economic reforms in the 1990s was to bring banks back from the brink. The RBI started a long process of aligning Indian banks with their global counter-parts — especially in terms of accounting and capital norms. The first capital adequacy rules that came into play the world over in the 1990s focused very heavily on credit risk. It was a binary approach, simplistic but useful. Lending to the private sector was risky and every such $100 loan had to be backed by $8 of bank capital. Lending to the government was riskless (in the sense that governments are unlikely to default on their domestic obligations). So a loan to the government did not need to be backed by capital.

This led to a new type of risk aversion, which made lending to the government more attractive than lending to the private sector. One of India's software czars once told me something interesting during a breakfast meeting. He said that the top four software companies in India had generated Rs. 28,000 *crores* in revenues, 170,000 jobs and Rs. 200,000 *crores* in investor wealth without borrowing a single *paisa* from the banking system (this was in the middle of 2005). To him, this was proof of the enterprise of the software majors as well as a severe indictment of Indian banks.

Actually, this inertia is a symptom of a deeper malaise. The banking sector has, especially between 1998 and 2003, shied away from doing its primary job — lending to the commercial sector. It has preferred to put its money in government bonds. At one point of time in 2002, banks were buying government bonds with a gluttonous appetite. Nearly 45% of the funds at their disposal had been used to buy the securities that the government was selling to finance its deficit (India has seen a credit boom since 2005, as banks again started lending to companies and individuals).

Ironically, as I have noted earlier, this strategy did not harm banks. The RBI aggressively cut interest rates after 1999. The prices of bonds owned by banks soared. So banks made huge profits. Bond prices were like a rising tide that lifted all boats; it did not matter whether the bank in question was weak or strong — profits rose in every corner of the banking system.

Most banks used the money wisely. The mountains of bad debts that were a burden on bank balance sheets were blasted away. And many banks were also quick to raise cheap capital from investors hypnotized by rising equity prices. Bankers were happy.

What was good news for banks was, however, not necessarily good news for the rest of the economy. Industry associations cried foul. They complained that companies were being denied credit. The small guys were the worst affected. The big companies in India had cut their dependence on bank finance — by tightening working capital, using internal funds, and borrowing abroad. But smaller companies across the country choked because of a credit squeeze. The quest for safe lending had come to a stage where banks were not ready to fund commercial enterprise.

In December 2002, at the annual bank economists' conference in Bangalore, Rakesh Mohan, deputy governor of the RBI, criticized banks for their sloth. He coined an evocative phrase that has stuck — lazy banking. In 2000 and 2001, two economists from the Massachusetts Institute of Technology (MIT), Abhijit Banerjee and Esther Duflo, spent a few days visiting branches of "an Indian public sector bank with a reputation for efficiency."

Here is how they described their experience:

> "Everyone we met seemed busy and the managers sounded like they knew what they were doing. We did notice that everyone's desks were strewn with memos, circulars and bulletins, full of

instructions, exhortations and prohibitions, but we still thought this was going to be different."[7]

All this activity was misleading. Banerjee and Duflo found that in 64% of the cases they observed, the amount of credit a company got was exactly equal to what it got previously (that number was as high as 70% in 1999). And in 73% of the cases where credit limits were frozen, the sales of the client (and hence working capital needs) had actually gone up. "There is an almost gratuitous perversity about some of what goes on in an Indian bank," say the two MIT economists darkly.[8]

There are several ways to explain the era of lazy banking. Industry was in recession and lending to it would have been too risky. The best companies had restructured and cut their demand for bank loans. Bank officers were too scared of taking risks because of the fear of being raided by the Central Bureau of Investigation (CBI), the central government agency that had jailed some bankers for lending to suspect companies. On a more general level, the lack of proper credit information and few creditor rights meant that the incentive to lend was weak. There is a modicum of truth in each of these explanations.

Years of directed credit and political programs such as loan *melas* have given a bad name to the entire business of lending to the poor. Is this about to change? Some banks have taken the lead by trying to give loans to small businesses and, in a few pilot projects, even to the ostensibly unbankable poor. Will the market finally solve the issue of how to increase financial inclusion without sacrificing profits? A lot will depend on the innovativeness of India's banks. But banking reforms too will play a part. Will they encourage risk-taking or will they focus more on financial stability?

EXPERIMENTS IN BAREFOOT BANKING

Guntur is a small town in the southern Indian state of Andhra Pradesh, surrounded by tobacco and chilli farms. It is the place where one of the most interesting experiments on how to do banking business with the poor is being carried out. ICICI Bank, India's second-largest and most innovative bank, has set up a pilot project in Guntur that is a test case for its belief that providing financial services to the poor can be a big growth area for Indian banks.

ICICI Bank has set up a few ATMs in and around Guntur that are like no other. These ATMs are powered by solar technology (because power supply is erratic in many parts of India), are connected to the main hub using wireless technologies (because rural India is inadequately wired) and identify customers using biometric techniques such as fingerprinting (because of high rates of illiteracy). These ATMs have been installed at some of the local shops. The local shopkeeper is the bank's front-end. He dishes out the cash. The need to set up expensive bank branches has been bypassed.

ICICI Bank CEO K.V. Kamath says that rural India is the next growth horizon for his organization. Kamath and his team have already revolutionized Indian banking in one important way. Till the mid-1990s, banks lent almost exclusively to producers and the government. There was hardly any consumer finance. Kamath saw before most of his peers that there were immense opportunities to lend profitably to ordinary Indians. The interest rates on consumer loans were higher and the default rate was lower. There has been a boom in consumer finance since then, as the middle-class borrowed to buy cars, TVs, and homes. Growth rates have consistently topped 50% a year.

But lending to the urban and rural poor is going to be far more difficult. Kamath succinctly defined the problem for me in a recent meeting. He said that the challenge is the small amounts of money involved. The average bank deposit in urban India is a tenth of the average bank deposit in a rich country. The average bank deposit in the rural areas will be a tenth of the average bank deposit in urban India. In effect, bankers will have to figure out how to handle bank accounts that are a hundredth of what the global banks handle, and do so profitably.

Banks like ICICI Bank have realized that this calls for innovativeness and unorthodox solutions. Banking costs have to drop by about 75% if banking with the poor is to be profitable. One way out is to work with civil society organizations that already have a presence in the rural areas. ICICI Bank has tied up with many self-help groups run by women. Each brings its unique strengths to the partnership. The self-help groups know the creditworthiness of their members and hence act as the front end for ICICI Bank's microlending initiatives. The bank uses its financial strength to raise money cheaply. It is a neat arrangement. If it works, it will undoubtedly be a role model for others (besides self-help groups, banks can also ride on other organizations that have a rural reach — like seed and fertilizer companies that do business with farmers).

Kamath told me that rural banking would grow in two waves. First, banks would lend to those who were denied bank credit till now, and thus help them generate wealth. Then, once these previously poor farmers and traders have the money to buy consumer goods, there will be a follow-up revolution in rural consumer credit.[8]

What banks like ICICI Bank are trying to do is both interesting and important. However, it is not yet clear how successful they will be. Part of the problem is that the success of these various initiatives does not depend merely on how well banks go about their job. A whole lot of other things have to fall in place — from more free markets for agricultural goods to better property rights. Yet, an increase in the degree of financial inclusiveness is a dire need in India. More people need to be given access to credit. The trick is to do it profitably. That will be what the coming revolution in Indian finance will really be all about. In its effect on Indian society and economy, it will have far greater implications than most people realize.

NOTES

1. "Reforms, Productivity and Efficiency in Banking: The Indian Experience", by Rakesh Mohan, 2005, available at: http://www.rbi.org.in.
2. "The Twin Crises: The Causes of Banking & Balance of Payments Problems", by Graciela L. Kaminsky and Carmen M. Reinhart, *American Economic Review*, June 1999.
3. G. Balachandran, *The Reserve Bank of India*, Vol. 3, 1967–1981, RBI, Mumbai, 2006.

Chapter 7

The Yogi and the Consumer

There is a fascinating story in one of the classical Hindu texts that throws light on key existential dilemmas. A man is running hard to escape a hungry tiger. He tumbles in panic and rolls off a precipice. He is falling to what promises to be a certain death in the gorge below, when he just manages to clutch at a small tree that is growing on the rock face. He hangs there for dear life. The choice is a bleak one. Above him is a hungry tiger and below him is a deep gorge. There is death on both sides. Just then, the dangling man's eyes fall upon an abandoned beehive that is a few feet above the tree that he is frantically hanging on to. There is honey dripping from the beehive. The man shuts his eyes and puts his tongue out to catch the sweet honey. It is his moment of fleeting bliss!

Now what does one make of this wonderful parable of existential dilemma? There are two possible explanations. The first is that humans are a contemptible lot. Here is this man facing a certain death and, even then, all he can think of is petty gratification of his senses. The story purportedly shows what trivial levels men can sink to in the face of important challenges. The other explanation is that the human condition is hopeless anyway. We are caught between the tiger and the gorge. It is the drops of honey that make our lives worth living. We maintain our humanity by aspiring to enjoy the little sensory pleasures.

I have heard both interpretations of the old fable being ardently defended. The point of telling this tale is to show that India has a far more ambivalent attitude toward material pleasure than is generally admitted. There are parallel traditions of

121

self-denial and enjoyment running through the centuries in Indian culture, as is only to be expected in any country with a long history and deep traditions. The monochromatic image of the mystic Orient was actually a convenient Occidental myth, once used to justify the colonization of the natives. In a neat twist, it is now a marketing tool used by spiritual entrepreneurs from the East to attract rich kids in London and Los Angeles. Actually, the inconclusive message of the fable of the tiger and the gorge shows that there has been a healthy struggle between the two competing world views stretching back many centuries into India's classical age. We have seen this essential tension play itself out in recent decades as well. The years of the freedom struggle and early independence were, under the influence of Mahatma Gandhi, years of pious austerity. The socialist era too discouraged conspicuous displays of wealth and success (it was quite another matter that the most enthusiastic proponents of simple living often went home to their Scotch whiskeys). All this has now changed beyond belief. You only have to spend an hour in a coffee shop or a mall in any Indian city to realize how the new generation of Indians is breaking away from the old culture of abstinence and glorified poverty.

Traditionalists may frown at the new materialism, but they may well be fighting a losing battle. Part of the reason is the changing demographics. Already, more than half of India's population has been born after 1980. These are kids who have grown up in a more consumerist India, with cable TV at home and goodies in the shops. They have no time for the fear and contempt for material success that captured the imagination of their parents' generation. They are the children of the reform era.

The shifting currents of social attitudes may seem completely out of place in a book on the Indian economy. But that is not so. If the new spirit of aggression that has taken Indian companies into global markets is an indication of how the animal spirits of one set of economic agents (entrepreneurs) have been unleashed over the past decade, the change in popular attitudes toward money and material pleasures points to something similar happening with another set of economic agents (consumers). The image of a young urban couple flashing their credit cards or of a rich trader's son in his gleaming new SUV does not merely reflect social pretentions. It reflects an economic reality as well.

LIGHTS, CAMERA, AND ACTION!

One way to gauge the change in attitudes, especially in urban India, is to look at a few films coming out of the cinematic factories of Mumbai. The film industry in India has its artistic roots in the progressive art movements that grew out of the antifascist and communist fronts in the 1930s and 1940s. In a country with scores of languages and dialects, Hindi films have been a cultural adhesive linking different parts of the country together with a common cultural idiom. The traditional ideology of Hindi films has been mildly socialist. I can scarcely remember a single Hindi film from 1950s and 1960s that did not flay the rich. If he was not a dacoit, then the bad man in a regular Hindi film was very likely to be a rich fellow who crushes the honest working class under his feet. This rather simplistic moral compass is now shifting, a reflection of the fact that India too is changing.

In a brilliant column written in 2001, Shekhar Gupta of the *Indian Express* newspaper wrote this about *Dil Chahta Hai*, a film about three footloose friends and their quest for love and meaning in their lives, which had a successful run in the cities:

> "Here all of them and their women are rich. They (including the women) drink champagne and wine. They happily ditch old boy/ girlfriends and hitch on to new ones. They flaunt the symbols of affluence: cellphones, resort holidays in Goa, 51-inch flat-screen televisions. They ride a Merc now and a Lexus then, drink beer from the bottle while driving and yet use seat-belts. When was the last time you saw a Hindi film that was so relaxed, so non-judgemental, so in-your-face about being rich?"

"If popular cinema mirrors the mind of our society," asks Gupta,

> "are we seeing the first stirrings of a post-reform urban India that is not embarrassed about being wealthy, where the rich are not wretched by implication and the poor, similarly, spiritually so well endowed? Too early to jump to that conclusion, perhaps, but there is no harm thinking that thought because unless that change comes about in the traditional Indian view of wealth and its creators, we have no real future except to become a colony of China."[1]

Or take another hit film of the first decade of this century, *Bunti Aur Babli*. It is a crime caper, loosely inspired by *Bonnie and Clyde*, the cult 1960s film that starred Warren Beatty and Faye Dunaway. The protagonists — a boy and a girl — get drawn into a series of scams that take them and their pursuers across India. The subtext of the film too is interesting. Both the charming young scamsters come from small-town India, and are desperate to break out of their claustrophobic surroundings.

Bunti is the son of a petty official in the Indian Railways. His father wants Bunti to emulate him and take a job in the railways. The boy dreams of becoming a "Tata-Birla-Ambani." His mind is bubbling with madcap schemes, but the important thing is that he wants to try to be like India's three largest business families (the Tatas, the Birlas, and the Ambanis). Then there is Babli, the small-town girl. Her parents want to get her married off. She wants to take part in beauty pageants and become Miss India. Her clothes are garish and her English is imperfect, but she wants to be there on the ramp with the hip big city girls. They both share an obsessive urge to make it big.

Both *Dil Chahta Hai* and *Bunti Aur Babli* held a mirror to the way attitudes are undergoing a sea change in urban India, especially amongst the youth. The goal of life is no longer a job in the railways or a marriage into a good family, let alone sitting cross-legged on a yoga mat. Money and material success are less likely to send their owners into paroxysms of guilt. Some of the new fascination for money does take crude forms, but to focus on that alone is to miss the point that films like *Dil Chahta Hai* and *Bunti Aur Babli* make. Interestingly, the young directors of both the films come from respected artistic families that have been on the left of the political spectrum. So one can safely assume that they are not insensitively celebrating nihilistic consumerism or petty crime in their films.

THE NEW AMBITIONS

Trying to capture social changes through cinematic filters can be an effective but imprecise undertaking. Trend spotters love to keep a sharp eye on the messages hidden in popular culture, including cinema. There is some method in the madness. But are there not other ways, based on hard numbers? Although it is not always an easy task, we can often glean some clues about the changes in social attitudes from economic data as well. Here is a whistle stop tour through some trends, chosen in a sadly random manner, which can give us advance information about the changes in many parts of India's complex social terrain.

The first point of call can be spending patterns in India. They are changing in tune with rising incomes, with expenses on food declining as a percentage of total private consumption expenditure and the share of expenses on items like communications, transport, education, and health going up sharply. Home ownership is on the rise. The census data shows that the number of households in India is rising faster than the total population, an indication that traditional joint families are splintering. Private debt is climbing very fast, though it is nowhere near the frightening levels one sees in the United States. Job-hopping has increased, with attrition rates in some industries (like software and outsourcing) touching 20%; the old paradigm of jobs held till retirement has been comprehensively junked.

Companies, especially those selling consumer goods, have still not quite figured out what these changes will mean for them. Nor has the political class. All one can say right now is that there is a curious combination of restlessness and confidence amongst the urban youth, at least the ones who have an education and a decent job. I suspect that these twin mindsets have spread to the young in other parts of Indian society as well. One often hears of young men in the villages who desperately want to escape the tyranny of marginal farming. The new generation of better-off farmers is likely to have had an education in an agricultural university, and can talk with great knowledge about new farming technology or global price trends in, say, sugar. (Not many know that the first truly networked community in India was not a major city or technology hub, but the sugar town of Warna and seventy neighboring villages in Western Maharashtra. They were wired by local initiative in 1999.)

The ambitions of young India are both promising and dangerous. Promising, because too much social energy has been wasted in India on trying to settle old grievances. The politics of caste and religion has, with some significant exceptions, been harmful. The interesting thing to look out for is whether the new economics translates into a new politics, striving for a better future rather than trying to settle old scores from the past. However, there is also a latent danger in the rising swell of expectations, because the dividing line between desire and resentment is often uncomfortably thin. A lot depends on whether the economy can perform well enough to fulfill desires and hence suppress resentment.

And nowhere do the new desires to get ahead in life reveal themselves so effectively than in the rise of educational aspirations in India. That, to me, is the definitive proof that India's social landscape is changing very fast. To millions of ordinary Indians, education is a private great leap forward.

THE IIT EFFECT

Kota is a medium-sized town in the desert state of Rajasthan that has been known throughout India for its traditional textiles and its stone (which is used for flooring in houses). Today, Kota has made a name for itself for another reason. It has become an education hub. Every year, around 30,000 students come to Kota to be trained to win what must be one of the hardest-fought educational battles in the world — admission to one of the seven elite Indian Institutes of Technology (IITs). Tens of thousands of students appear each year for the entrance exams that decide who will fill the 2,500 available seats. The training institutes in Kota say that a third of these seats are eventually filled by students who have been trained in the cram centers in their town.

The economy of Kota now revolves around the IIT entrance examinations. There are an estimated one hundred training institutes there. Till the early 1990s, the biggest employer in Kota was JK Synthetics, a textile firm that had a factory in the town. It employed 10,000 people. It closed in the early 1990s. Now, spending by the students holds up the economy. It is not just the training centers that benefit. Kota is dotted with around 200 eateries for the young wannabe engineers. Families keep aside a couple of rooms in their houses to rent out to these youngsters.

The doyen of the education economy in Kota is Vinod Bansal. He started off in the late 1980s by helping out three students in his dining room every evening. Muscular dystrophy paralyzed both his legs and eventually forced him to quit his job at JK Synthetics. Bansal concentrated on his tuition classes, and the business grew by leaps and bound. Today, he and his staff teach around 4,500 IIT aspirants every year in air-conditioned classes. It is said that tutors in Kota (most of them are IIT graduates themselves) often get paid salaries that are higher than those offered by even multinational companies. The fees, naturally, are pretty steep too.

The first IIT was set up in 1950 at Kharagpur, a military town in West Bengal. Then came the ones at Mumbai (1958), Chennai (1959), Kanpur (1960), Delhi (1961), Guwahati (1995), and the conversion of the engineering college at Roorkee into an IIT in 2001. The setting up of the IITs was one part of the ambitious attempt by Nehruvian India to develop a vibrant culture of science and technology in a country just emerging out of many centuries of foreign rule.

The magazine I work for once got an angry letter because it wrote that the college of engineering at Roorkee had been upgraded into an IIT. The writer took exception to the claim that his college had been "upgraded", which suggested that it was inferior to the IITs. He had a point: there is more to engineering education in India than the IITs. Yet, it is the IITs and the mad rush to get admitted to them that best captures the educational aspirations of the new India. The IITs are perhaps India's best-known brand name. They have been lavished with global press coverage, especially when there is the occasional scare about how India's technology gnomes will steal jobs from the West. Yet, there is far more to these wonderful technology institutes than the salaries and jobs that their alumni get.

The IITs (as well as their cousins, the Indian Institutes of Management — the IIMs) have been very effective vehicles for the democratization of Indian society. They have redefined the concept of the professional elite in India. Till the 1960s, Indian companies were quite prepared to employ amiable fools as long as they came from the right families, went to the right schools and could speak English with the right accent. This was a bit like the City in London before the Big Bang reforms of 1986. Vintage merchant banks would employ public school boys to man the dealing rooms. It was a world of leisurely lunches, clubby deals, and fat margins. India had a variant of this culture, especially in the old colonial firms with their stately dining rooms and liveried butlers. This "boxwallah" culture has been both celebrated and lampooned in India.

The rise in the importance of the IITs and the IIMs has changed that. Their graduates get the best jobs. And you cannot get into any of these institutes because of whom you know or how well you speak. Admission is largely based on ability, though the Indian government decided in the middle of 2006 to reserve some seats in the IITs and the IIMs for students from certain castes, thus shifting the admission process away from pure merit. In effect, the best jobs in the corporate sector have been thrown open to young professionals from every stratum of society. Education has become a springboard for thousands of smart kids across the country not born with the metaphorical silver spoon in their mouth.

Take the infamous case of Satyendra Dubey, a 31-year old engineer who was gunned down by hired killers in the badlands of Bihar in north India. Dubey was working with the National Highways Authority of India (NHAI), one of India's most effective government organizations that was then starting off on an ambitious plan to link India's four major cities with four-lane highways. The NHAI had made progress at a rate unknown in the country. And then Dubey was shot dead on November 27, 2003.

It was later revealed that Dubey had written a letter to the prime minister's office alleging corruption in the awarding of the contracts to build the highways. Many believe the letter was leaked and Dubey became a marked man. His killing led to a national uproar. It became a Big Story for the press. Among the interesting details to come out in the papers was Dubey's background. His father was a clerk in a tiny village in the state of Bihar, one of India's most backward parts. The family lived in a modest house. Dubey had his early education in the village school. And he had graduated from an IIT.[2]

There are not too many people in India who can match Dubey's moral courage. But he is quite typical in another way. He is one of a new generation in small town and rural India that aspires to get the best education and make their mark in the outside world. It is these ambitions that bring 30,000 IIT hopefuls to Kota every year.

PRIVATE SCHOOLS IN SLUMS

Educational aspirations are rising in India at a rate that has taken just about everybody by surprise. I have already written about the increase in school attendance figures across the country in the past 10 years. That trend alone gives us some idea of how poor Indians now realize that education is now an essential tool of empowerment. Additionally, there is a growing wave of private schooling in India — not just the faux-colonial snob schools in the hills but also basic schools in poor neighborhoods. Not all these private schools provide great education, but they inevitably charge fees that are far more than those charged by subsidized government schools.

Yet, they are attracting droves of students. Poor parents are ready to pay to educate their children, since they believe what often passes for an "English education" will help boys and girls get decent jobs. The issue right now is not the quality of education on offer. The readiness of poor parents to pay market rates for schooling is perhaps the most significant indication of rising aspirations in India.

James Tooley, a professor of education policy at the University of Newcastle, has written extensively of private schooling in India (and some other poor countries as well). The southern Indian city of Hyderabad has come into prominence for its ability to attract investments from global technology companies. It hopes to be the next Bangalore, and has been dubbed Cyberabad by the tech brigade. However, a third of the city's population lives in the crowded Old City, a pressure cooker of decrepit houses and narrow streets. Many of the people jammed into the Old City are poor.

Tooley and his team found private schools mushrooming all over this part of Hyderabad. Of the 918 schools they studied, 35% are run by the government, 23% are private schools that have been recognized by the government and another 23% are private but unrecognized schools. Another 5% are schools that are only private in name — they are completely funded by the government. Tooley calls schools in the unrecognized private schools category "a black market in education, operating entirely without state funding and regulation."[3] Now black markets can be seen as a moral problem. Or, more realistically, they can be recognized for what they are — private attempts to bridge the gap between the demand and supply of a particular good or service whose availability is smothered by government regulation.

The unrecognized private schools in Hyderabad are a response to the inability of the state to meet the growing demand for education in India. When Tooley and his team undertook their research some years ago, some 40% of the unrecognized schools were less than five years old, which is some indication of how the urge to send children to school is a relatively new phenomenon among poor families in urban India. The tuition fees in private schools in the poor parts of Hyderabad are not very steep. They average between $1.51 per month to $2.12 per month. Yet, they are quite steep considering the low incomes in the area. Tooley estimates that a typical family sending children to a private school parts with about 7% of its monthly earnings to pay for the education. That, for families that often experience hunger, is a remarkable fact.

Are the higher fees worth it? Several studies have shown that students going to private schools tend to get a better education compared to those who go to government schools. I could go on about whether private schools should be encouraged or whether the state should reclaim its role of educating every citizen. But that would be beside the point right now. What is more relevant to our current discussion is this: the growth of private schools that attract poor students, despite charging relatively stiff fees, is an important indication of how ordinary Indians are no longer satisfied with their current state. They aspire to a better life.

THE PERIPATETIC INDIAN SEES THE WORLD

India recorded its first "tourism deficit" in 2003. This means that the number of Indians going abroad was more than the number of foreigners coming into India that year. Close to five million Indians travel abroad every year. Never before have so many Indians had a chance to see the rest of the world. There are many reasons why millions, who live in a country with an abiding fear of crossing the seven seas, have suddenly become peripatetic: incomes have gone up, the rupee has been stable and the airline price wars have ensured that tickets on international flights have become cheaper by the year, thus ensuring that it is often cheaper to fly abroad than within India.

I was at the Bangkok airport at the end of January 2003, waiting to catch a flight home. There was a crowd of fellow Indians milling near the gate where our plane would dock. They were part of a large tour group that had been taken around Thailand, Malaysia, and Singapore. I got talking to two retired couples that had just finished their first international holiday. What one of the four said was instructive. He said they had been taken aback when they first saw cities like Bangkok, Kuala Lumpur, and Singapore. The roads, the buses, the buildings, the cleanliness — these Asian cities were miles ahead of comparable cities in India. They had not expected it. "Forget London and New York. Why can't we at least have cities like Kuala Lumpur?" one of them asked me. The four seniors were going home with a sense of how far India has been left behind by the neighbors to its east.

Lee Kuan Yew, Singapore's minister mentor and architect of its amazing makeover, has recounted a similar story in an interview with the German newspaper *Der Spiegel*. The visitor to these cities was Deng Xiaoping, the architect of China's makeover in 1980s and 1990s. Deng had just outmaneuvered the radical Gang of Four and had become China's supreme leader. In 1978, he visited Bangkok, Kuala Lumpur and Singapore. "I think that visit shocked him because he expected three backward cities. Instead he saw three modern cities and he knew that communism — the politics of the iron rice bowl — did not work," said Lee.[4] It was Deng's moment of epiphany.

I like to think that millions of Indians traveling abroad every year have similar revelations about how India has been left behind by the rest of Asia. It is easy to rationalize the gap between, say, London and Kolkata. You could argue that one was built with the colonial loot from the other. But how do you explain away the change in Kuala Lumpur — a city that, like Kolkata, is Asian, tropical, multicultural, and was once part of the British Empire?

Education, travel, and cable television have made millions of Indians aware of the progress made not just in Europe and America, but in the rest of Asia as well. The bar of expectations has been permanently raised.

NOTES

1. "Ah, The Sweet Smell of Poverty" by Shekhar Gupta, *Indian Express*, September 1, 2001.
2. *Indian Express* fine coverage of the Satyendra Dubey case is available at: http://www.indianexpress.com.
3. "Private Schools For The Poor: A Case Study From India", by James Tooley and Pauline Dixon (2003) available at: http://www.ncl.ac.uk/egwest/tooley.html, the homepage of Tooley.
4. Interview with Lee Kuan Yew in *Der Spiegel*, August 8, 2005.

8

Reforms for the Poor: The Acid Test

There are still about 250 million poor people in India. One reason why a quarter of a billion people continue to languish in poverty is that they have not benefited from economic reforms. This does not mean that they have been harmed by the opening up of the Indian economy, as some of the more militant opponents of liberal economics claim. The unstated assumption behind the claim that the poor have been harmed by economic reforms is that India's poor were once comfortably placed, before liberalization and globalization destroyed their livelihoods with heartless intent. That is nonsense. Poverty has been a persistent problem, predating economic reforms. It needs to be addressed in the very same way that it has been addressed elsewhere in the world: with capital, productivity and markets.

This is what the next round of economic reforms will have to concentrate on. Pundits often behave as if the task of freeing the Indian economy is now almost finished, other than a few tricky issues like privatization of government enterprises, getting foreign investment into select sectors like insurance, retail, and banking, and making the labor market more flexible. If only it was so easy. There has been a lot of progress on the grand macroeconomic issues such as tax reform, low tariffs, flexible exchange rates, etc. But that is the tip of the iceberg, easily seen by everyone. There is still an awesome mass of problems below the surface, and they can sink an economic Titanic.

Take the legal system, for example. Economist Bibek Debroy has closely studied the legal mess in India. "The legal system must provide an adequate structure of incentives and deterrents for a market-based economy to function. Globalisation also requires a legal system that conforms to global norms. Measured by this yardstick, the Indian legal system falls short," writes Debroy.[1] He once counted 45 central laws pertaining to labor. With that comes a welter of definitions and interpretations. Very often, discretionary powers are given to the local factory inspector to decide whether labor laws are being honored. This opens up immense possibilities of harassment and corruption — the "inspector raj" that businessmen often talk about.

But it is not the established businessman who is most affected by all this. He can fight or, more likely, pay his way out and put down the *baksheesh* as a hidden cost of business. It is the poor who suffer most from the restrictions and the ensuing corruption. They often do not have the money to pay off marauding local bureaucrats and policemen. Or else, the bribe is a very large proportion of their meager incomes. A hawker on a city street who pays a couple of hundred rupees to the policeman is giving up perhaps a tenth of his income to ply his trade. To him, it is a matter of livelihood rather than a mere business irritant.

THE NATURE OF INDIAN POVERTY

The acid test of economic reform is whether it can directly benefit the poor by increasing their ability to earn, rather than indirectly helping them through some glacial trickle-down process or through welfare handouts born out of a sense of pity. Reforms for the poor: it is not a smart slogan but an attractive possibility. Unfortunately, not much has been done on this front as yet, either by the government or by the private sector.

One way to look at the problem of persistent poverty in India is with the help of an apparent paradox: the unemployment rate is around 8%, while the poverty rate is 26%. It means that nearly one out of every five Indians is trapped in jobs that do not yield enough income to buy two square meals a day. Now why is this a paradox? Unemployment and poverty rates tend to march hand in hand in the rich countries. An employed person in the United States or Europe or Japan is likely to live outside the bleak circle of poverty. It is the unemployed who are poor. It is not so in India. You will see the *employed* poor wherever you look — the manual workers digging trenches along city roads with nothing but a few crude tools, the migrant families who walk from village to village looking for work during the harvest season, the marginal farmers scratching out a living on a small piece of dry land. It is a life of mud, sweat, and tears. These people are not poor because they do not work. They are poor because they are not productive enough. And they often do not have the means to be more productive. Thus, the challenge of poverty in India is actually a challenge of productivity.

There are two ways to attack the twin problems of poverty and low productivity. First, the government needs to remove restrictions on many sectors that have very high employment potential for those with few skills; sectors that can provide decent wages for a hard day's work. Organized retailing and construction are two obvious examples. Second, the poor have to have better access to capital, technology, information, property rights, and markets — the nuts and bolts of a modern market economy. The blanket of controls that suffocated the Indian economy has not been completely lifted as yet. Economic freedom is still restricted. And it is the poor who often bear the brunt of these restrictions, both directly and indirectly. Providing the poor with these basics of economic empowerment will require nothing less than a third wave of economic reform.

THREE WAVES OF ECONOMIC REFORM

India has experienced two major waves of economic reform till now — in the 1980s and in the 1990s. The first wave was focused on domestic liberalization. The basic idea was to give domestic industry greater freedom to invest and grow. The worst aspects of industrial licensing were junked. Exports were encouraged. Yet, competition continued to be severely restricted. Industrial licensing was still used to regulate the supply of output in the economy. New entrants continued to be frowned upon. And protectionist barriers were left untouched, which meant that Indian companies did not have to bother about competition from imports. So, in effect, the first wave of economic reform in India helped Indian business houses, especially the existing ones. The incumbents could increase their market power and protect their fat profit margins. It was reform for the established order.[2]

The second wave of economic reform was launched in 1991, after a financial crisis that almost forced India to default on its foreign debt obligations. The changes introduced in the years immediately after the crisis were more far-reaching than anticipated. Industrial licensing was abolished in one swift stroke, which meant that the barriers faced by new entrants disappeared suddenly. What is more, the long process to dismantle high tariff barriers began in earnest. Indian industry faced serious foreign competition for the first time in perhaps a hundred years. The beneficiaries of reform this time around were generally not producers, but consumers. The quality of goods improved dramatically and prices fell. Companies had to learn to live with more competition and lower profit margins. It was no surprise that some of the stiffest opposition to the second wave of economic reform in India came from the established industrial conglomerates, who realized that their old days of comfortable monopoly power were coming to an end.

These two waves of economic reform helped millions of Indians. But they also left many untouched. There is now a clear need for a third wave of economic reform in India, which will touch the lives of those who have not benefited from the first two waves. The benefits of economic reform have still not reached large parts of the country. Some would believe that it is in the nature of a market economy to create a deep divide between the haves and the have-nots; hence the temptation to throw money at the poor in the name of social justice. But there is another alternative: giving the poor certain basic economic powers so that they too can benefit from involvement in the modern market economy.

HAVE PITY ON THOSE WHO WANT TO TRADE IN RICE

It is quite clear to all but the most rigid antiglobalization ideologues that participation in the global economy has benefited India. The signs that India is a country on the move are unmistakable: consumers are spending like never before, companies are investing in new capacity, the planes landing every night bring in hundreds of foreign investors trying to find a profitable investment opportunity or two, every major city now resembles a huge building site. Even the popular irritants like traffic gridlocks and power shortages are indications that demand has raced ahead of supply because of a buoyant economy.

There can be little doubt that the long march from a controlled economy towards a market economy has lifted economic fortunes in India. Real incomes have almost doubled in the 15 years since 1991. The proportion of Indians living below the poverty line too has dropped very sharply. The debate on economic policy has changed spectacularly over the past 10 years. The animated sparring duels of today are not about the direction of change but about its pace. One happy result of fluctuating political fortunes is that just about every political formation in India has had a crack at governance in recent years. And once in government, everybody has quickly abandoned their erstwhile slogans and veered round to the consensus view that private enterprise, markets, and trade should have fewer restrictions in India.

The problem is that not every Indian has had equal access to the global economy. Successive prime ministers have made pious statements on how the economy needs to grow at 10% a year for a more aggressive attack on poverty to succeed. The supporting cast of finance ministers and economists follow with policy prescriptions that range from raising savings and investment rates to trying harder to attract foreign investment. Though all this is not off the mark, the debates on how India can lift its growth rate and bring down poverty fail to address the first principles: free markets, secure property rights and access to information.

Most Indians work in agriculture and in the informal sector. Here, they are often denied access to the basic economic rights that can help them participate in the global economy and prosper. Productivity levels are abysmal. This is both a problem and an opportunity, since the potential for large productivity gains on the farm, the corner shop and the neighborhood workshop is there right below our noses.

Economists have often argued that it is the differences in productivity that explain a large part of the differences in per capita national incomes. The opportunities for discontinuous jumps in productivity are not adequately appreciated in India. William W. Lewis, founding director of the McKinsey Global Institute, has shown that illiterate Mexican immigrants employed to build houses in Texas achieve world-class levels of productivity in almost no time. Workers in the Maruti Suzuki car plant in North India have productivity levels that are about 55% of their Japanese counterparts.[3] The average Indian worker, on the other hand, has productivity levels that are a mere 18% of a worker in developed markets. How can the gap be bridged quickly? White argues that it is competitive product markets that make a difference. They help lift productivity levels in an economy.

The wholesale rice trade is one illustration of how fettered markets still are in India. Economists Raghbendra Jha, KVB Murthy, and Anurag Sharma have done some interesting research on the restrictions on the wholesale rice trade in India. Here is what they say at one point in their paper:

> "There are controls and restrictions exercised by multiple authorities, at various levels. This results in serious barriers to trade at the inter-state and inter-district levels. There are differences in taxes and standards across the country. As a result of these restrictions and differentials the all-India market is fragmented. Traders are obliged to obtain licenses for trading and there are different authorities for issuing licenses for different goods. The process is highly time consuming, cumbersome, costly, variable and invariably corrupt. After obtaining a license the trader is faced with over 400 laws that govern trading. This plethora of restrictions and inherent differentials across the country prevent rational and uniform pricing strategies. The price differentials, in turn, do not reflect inherent market conditions and allow local scarcities to remain. The restrictions on trade prevent arbitrage possibilities, which could possibly help remove short-term price differentials."[4]

Four hundred laws governing trading in rice! Just to reiterate an earlier observation: economic reform has left large parts of the Indian economy untouched. It takes a lot of time and money to build roads to connect the hinterland to the urban and export markets. Removing legal restrictions on free trade, not just globally but also within India, is likely to be a far quicker way to boost productivity and incomes.

PROPERTY AND PROSPERITY: THE UNAPPRECIATED LINK

I was once working on a story of a government program to resettle Mumbai's slum dwellers, especially those who had been displaced by new road and rail projects. Builders had been invited to demolish the slums, house the slum dwellers in tiny 225 square foot tenements and develop the rest of the land commercially. It is a good idea based on a system of market incentives and the profit principle. The problem, as many urban activists told me then, was that the needs of the builder were overriding. He was the guy with the money. The urban poor would end up in soulless blocks of the type one sees on the outskirts of Moscow.

So why didn't the slum dwellers take charge and develop their area on their own? The problem: they were squatters who did not have clear rights to the property and hence no bank would finance them. The mortgage revolution that has helped the great Indian middle-class buy their own homes has left the urban poor untouched, because the rights to the collateral were in doubt. Clear property rights could have enabled at least some slum-dweller groups to raise money from banks, appoint their own architects and engineers, and rebuild their communities according to their own needs. The innovative Peruvian economist Hernando de Soto has written at length on how the lack of property rights means that the poor cannot convert their assets into productive capital. He estimates that the amount of dead capital in the world is more than $9.3 trillion!

I remember reading a very interesting story on this problem in the *Wall Street Journal*. It was about a slum on the other side of the word: Buenos Aires. Mercedes Almanda and Valentin Orellana are both residents of a barrio that was settled by poor families around 25 years ago. They have similar families and jobs. Yet, Almanda now lives in a comfortable brick house and her children have completed their educations. Orellana continues to live in a shack with a corrugated zinc roof and none of his children have completed school. Why? Matt Moffett, the writer of this instructive article, says the difference in the progress of the two families can be explained by one simple fact: land titles. Between 1989 and 1991, squatters in 419 lots in the barrio received land titles from the government. Then, because of a change in government, those on the other 410 lots did not. Almanda has a title to her house while Orellana does not. The family with property rights moved ahead, while the one without property rights was left behind.[5]

Economists often fret over the fact that they cannot observe controlled experiments as, say, physicists or biologists can. But the opportunity does crop up now and then. The tale of the two erstwhile Germanys is revealing. Both West Germany and East Germany shared the same characteristics in 1945: initial conditions, natural resource endowments, the people, cultural attitudes, weather, etc. The only significant difference was their economic systems. It is pretty clear that West Germany succeeded while East Germany collapsed because the former had the better economic system. Even today, the contrast between prosperous South Korea and starving North Korea is proof that markets work better than centralized plans. Similarly, what happened in that Argentine barrio shows why property rights are important, and how they can often be the one thing standing between poverty and a decent life.

Contemporary economic debate in India tends to be limited, if not outright sterile, because few seem to appreciate the importance of adequate and clear property rights. The pundits often claim that India is now almost through with the task of reforming its economy. The unfinished work is restricted to a few sensitive areas like privatization or foreign investment in select sectors like insurance, banking, and retail or the creation of flexible labor markets. That amounts to underestimating the task at hand. There is a dire need for a third wave of economic reform — and this wave will have to focus on the country's poor and their ability to participate in the modern global economy. Around 92% of India's total workforce of 370 million workers was employed in the informal sector in 2000, and they produce 70% of India's GDP and 40% of its exports. Given the sheer number of people involved and the huge potential for productivity gains in the informal sector, we could be talking about a tsunami rather than a mere wave.

A DIFFERENT DICHOTOMY

Is India really a free economy today? Or is it even becoming one rapidly enough? The answers to these questions are not simple, as may be thought. Large parts of the Indian economy are still in fetters. True, the government has been assiduously trying to replace its red tape with red carpets. Ministers and bureaucrats like to pretend that India is open for business. Local corporate titans now sit on government councils. Foreign business leaders are treated like visiting heads of state. Local governments do all they can to clear the way for large projects. I doubt that any other country gives the likes of Bill Gates the sort of fawning attention India gives him every time he comes visiting. Yet, this new enthusiasm for private enterprise, though welcome, extends to barely a tenth of the economy. This is the world of influential companies, both local and global. The deregulation of the Indian economy is largely for the people who meet at Davos every winter, who are friends with ministers and top bureaucrats and who can threaten to move their capital elsewhere if their concerns are not met.

Not everyone has it so easy, however. India has a long, long way to go before the vast majority of its people get similar levels of economic freedom. The small businessman who is harassed by factory inspectors, the farmer who is prevented from selling his produce in the next state, the roadside hawker who has to pay protection money to the police — they all continue to be tangled in all sorts of outdated restrictions that prevent them from creating wealth or seeking productive livelihoods. It is almost as if there are now two economies in India — one free and one shackled. And this is a painful dichotomy that many would prefer to ignore.

One of the most disturbing portrayals of the lack of economic freedom for the common Indian that I have seen is a study by the Center For Civil Society, a liberal think tank in New Delhi. Two young researchers, Kumar Gaurav and Mayank Singhal, took a detailed look at the economic lives of the porters who carry baggage at the city's three main railway stations. You cannot miss the porters at any railway station anywhere in India, in their red uniforms and their trademark metal badges that are tied to their arms. The porters are not employees of the Indian railways. They are independent professionals who are given licenses by the station authorities to ply their trade at various railways stations.

With licensing come all sorts of ills. These licenses are rationed, depending on demand projections for porter services made by the railways. New licenses are given out every three to four years by the station authorities. When the process for a new round of porter licenses was started in 2002 with newspaper advertisements, there was a huge rush of hopefuls — there were a hundred applicants for every one advertised license. Naturally, artificial scarcity has brought with it rent-seeking premiums and corruption. The premium on a license varied between Rs. 1.8 *lakh* and Rs. 4 *lakh*, which is several times more than what an average porter earns in a year. So why are porters ready to pay such stiff premiums to get their licenses? "Since the porter's license can be passed on from one generation to the next, it becomes a long-term secure investment where one can recover his money over a period of time," say Gaurav and Singhal.[6]

Not everyone transfers their license to family members. The ability to make a quick buck attracts arbitrageurs. They capture licenses and then sell them to others for a profit. The problem is that the licenses can only be transferred to members of one's own family and then only if the original license holder is no longer able to carry his load because of an illness or old age. So there is a parallel world of false medical certificates, touts, and cash transfers. Gaurav and Singhal noticed that in 2001, nearly 72% of the porter licenses that had been transferred went to brothers-in-law, rather than direct descendants like sons or nephews. They smelt a rat. It was quite clear that these brothers-in-law were fictitious family members. There were very few sons to carry the porter's mantle. The two researchers remarked wryly that it seemed as though "carrying a load on the head makes one impotent!"[7]

What happens at the railway stations in New Delhi is not unique. Vast parts of the Indian economy are still in the tight clutches of rules and regulations that hinder rather than foster work and enterprise. Ironically, even India's biggest companies had to live in a similar world about 20 years ago. They needed permission from the government to increase production, build new factories or get into new areas of business. The government in turn gave licenses only after its economists were convinced that there would be demand to absorb the new supplies. Those who could use political contacts to get licenses used them to earn monopoly profits. It was a shadowy world of inefficiency and corruption, of touts, lobbyists, and officials on the take, of rent-seeking and monopoly profits. Big business has been freed from these old insanities. The average business has not been so lucky. The benefits of deregulation have not reached it.

THE PAIN OF DOING BUSINESS IN INDIA

The average business enterprise in India is still burdened with all sorts of regulations and delays. I wrote large parts of this book sitting in an office of a telecom software company that has been started by a group of young engineers. They spend an inordinate amount of time getting various clearances. And remember: technology firms have a relatively easy time in India. The thousands of small companies in the industrial sector have to deal with many more varieties of bureaucratic tyrants — from tax officials to sanitary inspectors. Each wants his pound of flesh.

The World Bank brings out an excellent report every year on how easy or difficult it is to do business in various countries. India, despite all the economic reform since 1991, always ends up at the bottom of the tables. In 2005, for example, India was 116th among 156 countries.[8] In other words, it was one of the most difficult countries in the world in which to run a business. This merely confirms to the outside world what the average Indian businessman already knows. India's performance on individual parameters — starting a business, dealing with licenses, registering property, and hiring and firing — is awful.

Let us say you want to start a business in India. What will this mean? Of course, you will need a business plan and capital and machinery. After that comes the real difficult part. An entrepreneur who wants to start a new business in India has to go through 11 steps that take about 71 days. The cost of this entire procedure is about 61% of the income of the average Indian. Once the business is up and running, dealing with the various licensing regulations involves 20 procedures and 270 days. Here too, the costs are steep: 678% of average annual income to meet licensing regulations. In other words, the average Indian will find it extremely expensive to start and run an official business. And it takes an average of 10 years to close a business.

The point is a simple one. India has moved a great distance in terms of macroeconomic policies. It has junked its old system of industrial licensing, now has moderate tax rates, has encouraged foreign trade and has a more stable financial system. But on the ground, the situation has not changed fast enough. It continues to be bureaucratic and slow moving. It is far easier in China to start a new business, send goods to your export markets and register property. On the other hand, it is easier to fire workers and comply with licenses in India.

There is a reason why these difficulties on the ground are likely to hurt India more than China. It goes back to the structure of the two economies. India has a more entrepreneurial economy while China depends more heavily on large investments by multinationals. Domestic capitalism is more vibrant in India and hence the roadblocks to doing business have more serious implications. This is what the Swedish liberal writer Johan Norberg wrote after a visit to India at the end of 2005.

> "India's hidden strength is that the country is already extremely entrepreneurial — but in the informal sector. An Indian friend mentions that most of the cars we see on the roads, and many computers in the offices, are assembled in small, informal factories, outside the law, to avoid the many taxes and regulations that still curb the Indian economy. Imagine what the Indians could do if all that energy was legalized. In that case the Chinese have good reasons to see them as serious competitors."[9]

I am not quite sure what cars Norberg's friend was talking about, because as far as I know, Indians do not drive cars assembled in informal factories. But the general thrust of his argument is indisputable. The sheer weight of regulations either completely smothers grassroots enterprise in India or else drives large parts of it into the informal sector (Table 8).

Table 8
The Travails of Doing Business in India

	India	South Asia	Singapore
Starting a business			
Procedures (No.)	11	7.9	6
Time (days)	71	35.3	6
Cost (% of income per capita)	61.7	40.5	1.1
Dealing with licenses			
Procedure (No.)	20	15.7	11
Time (days)	270	195.3	129
Cost (% of income)	678.5	385.9	24
Trading across borders			
Documents for export (No.)	10	8.1	5
Signatures for export (No.)	22	12.1	2
Time for export (days)	36	33.7	6
Documents for import (No.)	15	12.8	6
Signatures for import (No.)	27	24	2
Time for import (days)	43	46.5	8
Closing a business			
Time (years)	10	4.2	1
Cost (% of estate)	9	7.3	1
Recovery rate (cents per dollar)	12.8	19.7	91.3

Source: World Bank.

THE POWER OF INFORMATION: PROJECT BHOOMI

The Indian farmer struggles against a variety of odds — capricious weather, lack of adequate credit from the official banking system, no infrastructure to help him get his goods to urban markets, often being forced to sell his produce in local markets rather than in markets where he can get the best price, tiny landholdings, and much more. And to make things even worse, there are the local government bureaucrats who are often inefficient and corrupt.

Till recently, the southern state of Karnataka maintained 20 million land records in a sea of paper that was spread across the state. A farmer who wanted to get a copy of a basic property document that is called his RTC (record of rights, tenancy and crops) had to go to the local village accountant with a request. There were 9,000 of these village accountants in Andhra Pradesh and each of them handled requests from a group of three or four villages. A farmer may want a copy of his RTC because he wanted to present it to the local bank before getting a loan. He may also want to change the details on this document after a change in ownership, either because of a sale or inheritance.

The traditional process could be excruciatingly slow. Requests for changes in RTCs had to be filed with the village accountant. These accountants were often traveling between the various villages they serviced, and hence were difficult to locate. Once an accountant got a request from a farmer to get the RTC altered, he would have to follow what looks like a simple process. He would contact those people who he thought could have objections to the change in ownership. He would also paste a public notice where many people could see it, which often meant the local post office. If nobody objected within a month, a revenue inspector would change the name on the RTC.

It looks pretty simple, but in actual practice the accountant and the revenue inspector could stall and force an increasingly desperate farmer to bribe his way out. The only other option would mean a wait for many months, often a year and more. A farmer without his RTC would find it impossible to get a bank loan. There was always a danger that some unscrupulous people would pay a higher bribe and get the property transferred to their name. There was no way to find out till it was too late. Land records were not open for public scrutiny. It was almost as if they were governed by the Official Secrets Act.

You will realize that I have written most of the previous few paragraphs in the past tense. The reason is Project Bhoomi, a landmark government program to computerize land records and make things easier for harried farmers in Karnataka (*Bhoomi* means land in many Indian languages, and this particular project is now being replicated in a few other Indian states). A farmer can today go to any of the computer kiosks (or Bhoomi centers) across the state of Karnataka. There is a full-time village accountant at hand near each of these kiosks. A farmer can get a copy of his RTC online by paying a small fee of Rs. 15. All he has to do is feed in either the name of the landowner or the plot number. A second screen shows the request being processed in real time.

Changes in the RTCs have become simple as well. A farmer can make his request online at any of the kiosks. He gets an application number and can later check the status of his application on a touch screen. The applications get forwarded to the relevant village accountant. The subsequent process of checking for objections from interested parties remains the same. But after that is done, the revenue inspector sends the changes in the RTC to the Bhoomi center, where a new document is created and scanned. The applicant can get a printout whenever he visits the centre next. The entire process is now transparent and fast.

Project Bhoomi is merely one of the most stunning examples of what modern communications technology can do for poor Indians. While the need to promote investments in rural areas and also the need to give farmers greater access to markets remain, digital tools can help reduce some of the problems that Indian farmers face. Take the case of Project Drishtee, another attempt to provide digital tools to the poor. The initiative is a private sector one, started in the central Indian state of Madhya Pradesh. The project website tells how farmers in Bagadi village in Dhar district used computers set up by Project Drishtee to compare potato prices in various markets. They were getting Rs. 300 per quintal from local traders so they shifted their produce to Indore, where they received Rs. 400 a quintal.

Or take the case of the fishermen of Kerala, a state at the southern tip of the Indian peninsula. Many of them have invested in a Global Positioning System (GPS) that allows them to identify fish-rich territories on the high seas. The fishing boats are in touch with the Navistar Satellite Constellation, consisting of 32 satellites circling the earth, to help them locate fish. Once the catch is hauled, regular mobile phones are used to negotiate prices with wholesale traders at various ports. The boats land at the port where the prices are highest.

UNEQUAL BENEFITS

Martin Bernstein, then the director of one of the museum shops at the Smithsonian Institution in Washington, DC, visited the desert city of Jodhpur in March 2000. He went to the showroom of Lalji, one of the biggest dealers in handicrafts in the city. Bernstein's eyes fell on row after row of brass globes that were made to resemble antiques. It was the quoted prices that took him by surprise. The wholesale price for each globe was $4.50, but it could have been beaten down by a hard bargainer. Bernstein had seen these pieces retailing at between $25 and $35 at the New York outlet run by one of Lalji's clients. What is more, Bernstein could have bought them at these steep prices and sold them at the museum shop for $70.

This little anecdote is from *Handmade In India*, an article by Maureen Liebl and Tirthankar Roy,[10] which carefully documents the handicrafts industry in India. The authors assume that Lalji pays his artisans about a dollar for every one of those brass globes that retail in Washington, DC at $70. A 70-fold difference between the price paid to the producer and the price paid by the final consumer is unheard of in more organized industries. What this shows is that the market infrastructure that is meant to intermediate between producers in Jodhpur and consumers in Washington, DC is woefully inadequate. Artisans do not have adequate market linkages, they are often denied working capital and their traditional knowledge and skills are not protected.

The lack of well-developed markets ensures that those who step in to plug the gap between producer and consumer can capture an unfairly large chunk of the value created. Prices may be particularly high when handicrafts are exported to different corners of the world. But the basic problem persists in the local markets as well. Liebl and Roy mention the case of Shyam Lal, whose family once did engraving and die-making exclusively for the royal family of Jodhpur. His products sell in the local Jodhpur market at three or four times the price at which he sells to dealers.

I had once been to Paithan, a temple town in the state of Maharashtra, which is famous for its *Paithani* sarees (at one point of time, British Airways had used *Paithani* design motifs on the tails of some of its planes). The famous handmade sarees made in Paithan are among the more expensive types produced in India. A local official had taken me to the home-cum-workplace of one couple that makes these sarees. As I was watching their deft craftsmanship, they explained the economics of making sarees in Paithan. It takes about six months to make one saree. The craftsmen buy the raw material at the beginning of this long production cycle and sell the saree when it is over. They have no cash earnings in the intervening period — nothing to run the household. So the artisans depend on local dealers who lend them money and buy the finished saree. The terms of trade are, naturally, beneficial to the dealers who then take the sarees to Mumbai and beyond. In a few cases, loyal customers come and buy a saree when it is still being worked on.

A comparison of traditional handicraft industries with India's successful software and outsourcing industries can be instructive. Both the weavers and the code writers use knowledge and skills to service distant markets. There are around five times more workers in informal industries than in the headline-grabbing technology companies. Yet, as Liebl and Roy note: "... the return on skill remains low, and markets still remain small and unstable. Weaknesses on the crafts producers, side limit the quality of goods, innovation etc. There is no development of links between local traditions and world markets."

THE POWER OF THE MARKET

The porters at New Delhi station struggling to get licenses, the farmers in Karnataka who used to find even the simple act of getting a property document so difficult, the rice farmers and traders who have to deal with a mountain of regulations, the handicraft workers who are paid a pittance compared to the prices that their products command in the fashion-conscious markets of the world — there is a common thread running through all these tales. The basic building blocks of a market economy are often not strong enough in their lives. Either there are silly restrictions on trade, lack of proper supply chains, inadequate access to capital, no information on prices ... the list is pretty long and worrisome.

The first principles of an open economy are often not met in many areas of the Indian economy. Millions are unable to take the great leaps in productivity and innovation that are needed to generate more incomes and wealth in the informal sector. Unfortunately, there is almost a conspiracy of silence around these issues in contemporary India. This is in no way a pointer to the "us-versus-them" variant of politics. My arguments are based on a simple fact — it is inconceivable that hundreds of millions of young Indians will all end up writing software code in Bangalore or taking phone calls in Gurgaon. Even the opportunities in large-scale manufacturing will be relatively modest. The average Indian is likely to be in an average job — growing vegetables, driving a truck, managing a neighborhood shop, or repairing cars.

The question is: do they have the freedom — to earn and invest — that large companies take for granted today?

NOTES

1. "Reforming The Legal System", by Bibek Debroy; available at: http://www.mayin.org/ajayshah/A/Debroy1.pdf.
2. The distinction between pro-business and pro-market reforms was first suggested in "From Hindu Growth To Productivity Surge: The Mystery of The Indian Growth Transition", by Dani Rodrik and Arvind Subramanian; IMF Working Paper 77 (2004).
3. "The Power of Productivity", by William W. Lewis, *McKinsey Quarterly* No. 2 (2004).
4. "Market Integration In Wholesale Rice Markets In India", by Raghbendra Jha, K.V.B. Murthy and Anurag Sharma; ASARC Working Paper 2005/03 (2005); available at: http://www.abareconomics.com/research/india/papers/ricemarketintegratnjha.pdf.
5. *Wall Street Journal*, November 9, 2005.
6. "Licensing of the Railway Porters: The Burden of the Badge", by Kumar Gaurav and Mayank Singhal; Working Paper 63; Centre For Civil Society, New Delhi (2003).
7. Ibid.
8. This data is available at: http://www.doingbusiness.org.
9. From http://www.johannorberg.net.
10. "Handmade in India: Traditional Craft Skills In A Changing World", by Maureen Liebl and Tirthankar Roy; in *Poor People's Knowledge* edited by J. Michael Finger and Philip Schuler; World Bank and Oxford University Press (2004); a text version is available at: http://www-wds.worldbank.org.

Chapter 9

The Dark Side of the Moon

India will have to deal with myriad challenges in the years ahead if it is to ensure that it remains on its current growth trajectory and also if it is to help more and more of its citizens become active participants in the global economy. Five issues stand out: poverty trends, income inequality, energy, employment, and infrastructure.

IS POVERTY INCREASING IN INDIA?

About 30 minutes away from Mumbai's swank new business district, the Bandra Kurla Complex, where some of the country's largest companies are headquartered in towers of glass and steel, is a nondescript little lane called *Machchhar Galli*. In the local language, it literally means "Mosquito Lane". Here, a rundown tenement block houses workers from the now-defunct Swadeshi Mills. This textile mill is part of the city's commercial folklore. It had been bought by pioneering industrialist Jamshetji Tata in 1886. In its days of glory, cloth produced in Swadeshi Mills was sold in distant markets like China, Korea, and Japan. The looms here stopped whirring after the mid-1980s.

Deepak Patil was one of the thousands of workers who were forced into idleness because of the slow decline of Mumbai's textile industry over the past 20 years. He worked for Swadeshi Mills and lived in *Machchhar Galli*. In the middle of 2003, Patil jumped in front of a suburban train and killed himself. The local newspapers reported what he wrote to his wife in the suicide note: "I am dying because my mill shut down." Other unemployed textile workers

151

just about manage to keep desperation at bay. A few of the more daring boys join criminal gangs.

Elsewhere, the heart of Mumbai's old textile district is being torn down and rebuilt to house fancy offices and apartments. Squalor and prosperity coexist here in an uneasy truce. And further away into the hinterland, there is the steady trickle of grim stories of villages that have been wrecked by capricious cycles of drought and floods; and of farmers who have embraced death by swallowing pesticide because of mounting debts. There have been cases of farmers selling their kidneys and other vital organs to earn money. The 270 residents of Dorli, a tiny hamlet in the state of Maharashtra, put their entire village on sale in 2006 — land, houses, and livestock. It is desperate measures such as these that have fed concerns that the benefits of economic reforms have not filtered down to the poor.

How justified are these concerns?

There is little doubt that the wave of corporate restructuring that lashed the country in the 1990s has been harsh on workers like Patil, as companies focused on cost cutting. It is also indisputable that millions of Indians still live on the edge of deprivation, a fact that is often unseen by investors blinded by India's roaring GDP growth rates. But the individual stories of distress — though tragic by themselves — do not quite add up to the giant, heartrending tale of rising poverty that circulates today. In fact, the cold data show that Indians are far better off today than they were in 1991, the year when radical economic reforms were initiated.

Economists love to argue that growth is the best antidote for poverty. India and China are the most dramatic test cases for this comforting hypothesis. India's economy inched ahead between 1950 and 1980. Average incomes rose by a mere 1.2% a year in this period of muddled socialism. Naturally, there was no perceptible decline in poverty during those stagnant decades. But since 1980, when the first tentative reform measures were undertaken, incomes have increased at around 4% a year, leading to huge drops in poverty (despite perhaps some increase in inequality). India's GDP growth has averaged over 6% between 1991 and 2005. Average incomes have increased by over 4% a year since 1991.

Poverty rates are calculated from the regular surveys conducted by the National Sample Survey (NSS). The 55th round of the survey was conducted in 1999–2000. It showed that the percentage of Indians living below the poverty line fell to 24% (compared to 36% in 1993–1994, the year the previous comprehensive survey was done). This means that 120 million Indians climbed out of poverty in six short years. The data thrown up by the 55th round of the NSS was controversial, however. It sparked off many academic battles because the method used for this survey was different from those used earlier. Hence the data was difficult to compare.

These battles are part of a wider disagreement about the actual trend of poverty in India. Some economists, like Raghbendra Jha of the Australian National University, say that poverty declines in the 1990s have been modest. Poverty declined at a faster rate in the 1980s. Leading the opposite charge is Oxus Research & Investment president Surjit Bhalla. His analysis shows that poverty has fallen far more than the NSS data shows. Bhalla says that only 12% of Indians lived below the poverty line in 1998. Jean Dreze and Angus Deaton's adjusted estimates show that rural poverty was 26.3% (as against 26.8% in the official NSS data) while urban poverty was far lower, at 12% (24.1% according to the NSS).[1]

These disagreements are part of a global war of numbers. The effect of economic reform and globalization on poverty is a hotly debated issue. The recent Indian debates about the extent of poverty declines are an echo of the larger, global debates. But what is significant is this: not one serious economist says that poverty has actually increased since 1991, in sharp contrast to what the more passionate opponents of globalization charge.

Once again, there are some individual cases where globalization has led to deprivation and suicide. About 800 km away from Mumbai is the cotton-growing region of Vidarbha, perched on the Deccan Plateau. Hundreds of cotton farmers here have killed themselves in recent years. The reasons are complex and varied. Among the reasons is this one: farmers here cannot compete with cheap cotton imported from the United States, whose farmers are lavished with huge subsidies by a government that preaches the virtues of competitive markets to the rest of the world. Their deaths can be linked to imperfect globalization. More generally, though, reform and globalization have led to faster growth and sharp drops in poverty levels.

THE WIDENING DIVIDE: A CAUSE FOR CONCERN?

And what about inequality?

When the economist Simon Kuznets studied the relationship between the level of development in a country and income inequality there, he came across a clear trend. Within the group of countries with low levels of income, the relatively better-off poor countries had higher levels of income inequality compared to the rest. On the other hand, the high-income countries showed the very opposite trend. Here, it was the ones that had relatively lower incomes that had higher levels of income inequality. This led to the creation of the famous Kuznets Curve — an inverted U that showed how income equality went up in the early stages of development and then came down as average incomes crossed a certain threshold. In short, initial bursts of growth tend to create greater income inequality.

Kuznets did his work on development and income inequality more than four decades ago, and many economists have subsequently tried to pick holes in his arguments. But Kuznet's central conclusion does assume great significance in any study of contemporary India. There are fears that a disproportionate part of the benefits of rapid economic growth have gone to a small minority. Income distribution is not a major political issue as yet, but it could become more important in the years ahead. China has already reached a stage when the wide divide between the coastal cities and the rest of the country is seen as a potential risk by both the economists and the party bosses.

There are telltale signs of growing inequality in India. The country today has 23 billionaires, more than China (with eight of them) and not far short of Japan's 27, according to *Forbes* magazine.[2] The annual surveys of global wealth by Merrill Lynch and Cap Gemini consistently show how the number of dollar millionaires (*70,000 at last count*) is growing very rapidly in India. Urban India has already seen successful young kids lavished with lucrative stock options and large bonuses. Companies today offer their top management salaries that were unheard of even five years ago. Spending on all sorts of luxury goods — from Swiss watches to gourmet meals — has soared in recent years.

The precise way to measure income inequality is through the Gini coefficient. The income data in India is inadequate, and there have been messy debates on the exact trend in income inequality in recent times. There are three economic trends that suggest that there is a widening chasm in Indian incomes, more or less as Kuznets predicted.

First, there are the trends in consumption. Some analyses of consumption data show that the poor are consuming less than before. Abhijit Sen of Jawaharlal Nehru University argues that spending on food (as a percent of total private spending) has fallen by 6% since 1999 and the contribution of items such as fuel, health, education, and transport has increased over the same period because employment has remained flat. Most of the increase in incomes has gone to people who are already employed and who cannot spend beyond a certain point on more food.[3]

Second, consider the trend of an increasing tax-to-GDP ratio since 2003 (after more than a decade of decline), which could also contain hints about growing income inequality. More tax can be collected per unit of GDP if either tax rates are increased or if more citizens are brought within the tax net. In India, tax rates have fallen; so the first explanation is clearly of no use. There is no doubt that more people pay taxes in India today, and that could be a major factor behind the rising tax-to-GDP ratio. But there is a third factor: are tax collections going up because a larger part of India's national income is going to the rich and to companies?

Finally, the sudden spike in the savings rate too could indicate that income inequality is increasing. India's savings rate, which hovered around 24% of its GDP through the 1990s, suddenly took wing in the first years of the new century. It is now a few whiskers away from touching the 30% mark. There are many obvious reasons why the savings rate is going up, one reason being that the government has started putting its finances in order and this has obliterated public sector dis-saving. Growing income inequality too could be a factor here. Some Keynesian economists like Nicholas Kaldor have argued that the propensity to save from profits is higher than the propensity to save from wages. The sudden spike in savings in India could be because corporate profits are accounting for a larger portion of India's GDP than before.

So while there is no conclusive proof, it is likely that income inequality has been inching up in India. Why is inequality growing and is it a major cause for concern? Jha mentions three reasons why inequality could have gone up (particularly in urban areas). One, the relative share of national output going to capital (as against labor) has gone up; two, the rate of labor absorption has declined; and three, the services sector has grown rapidly. Every society has some level of inequality. It is very difficult to judge what a tolerable level of inequality is. It is a moot question whether inequality in India would increase to Latin American levels and create deep rifts within society. But a little rise in inequality is not necessarily a bad thing, because it can act as an incentive for hard work.

What is more crucial at this stage is the trend in absolute levels of poverty. Should India concentrate on faster growth and tolerate marginal increases in inequality? Arvind Panagariya of the University of Maryland has outlined three key reasons why growth is so crucial to poverty reduction. First, when per capita incomes grow at more than 3% a year, the effects of an increase in inequality "are overwhelmed." Second, faster growth means there is more money to finance various antipoverty schemes. Third, growth improves the ability of the poor to access public services.[4]

At this juncture, India would be better off trying to address the problem of absolute poverty rather than bothering too much about marginal increases in inequality. What matters more is what the poor are actually consuming rather than how much less they are consuming compared to the rich. The real challenge is to ensure that the incomes of the poor do not stagnate or drop; that would be a social disaster. Sundeep Waslekar of The Strategic Foresight Group, a think tank, has pointed out a disturbing dichotomy — the Maoist movement in the tribal areas has gained support at precisely the same time that economic growth took off in India.[5] Think about it.

THE ENERGETIC WASTE OF ENERGY

The Rashtrapati Bhavan is the official residence of the President of India. It is one of the grandest homes in the world — a colonial palace of 200,000 square feet and 340 rooms. Rashtrapati Bhavan was built in the second decade of the 20th century to house the Viceroy of India in the days of the British Raj. The person living in this majestic building at the beginning of the 21st century is A.P.J. Abdul Kalam, an accomplished scientist and the 11th President of the Indian republic. This remarkable man has done a lot to reach out to the people of India — through his letters to children, his personal website, his friendly, and distinctly non-presidential demeanor.

Kalam likes to set an example. He got an energy audit done for his official residence and has given a commitment to cut energy consumption at Rashtrapati Bhavan by 23%. He has even planned an 8 MW solar energy plant in his estate to make it self-sufficient in energy. There are no signs that Kalam's example will be picked up by the rest of the country. India continues to be one of the most profligate users of energy in the world — a dangerous habit for a country that imports about 70% of its petroleum (oil imports are expected to account for 90% of India's total oil consumption by 2020).[6]

Has the larger point behind the President's initiative — that energy needs to be used more intelligently — been lost on India's energy establishment? In the autumn of 2004, oil was once again on the boil. Prices were nudging towards $50 a barrel and the world was headed for what is now seen as the third great oil shock. The two previous ones — in 1973 and 1979 — had brought the global economy to its knees. India too had been hit hard by low growth and high inflation. In 1973, GDP fell by 0.3% and inflation climbed to 20.2%. In 1979, GDP fell by 5.2% and inflation was up at 17.1%. What is more, the short but sharp spike in oil prices during the first Gulf War in 1990 led to capital flight and a balance of payments crisis.

The third oil shock has been different — at least in the initial period. The Indian economy has continued to coast along at an average rate in excess of 7% a year. Inflation has generally been down at around 5%. But that is not the only thing that makes the third oil shock interesting. For the first time in history, oil analysts and economists were fretting about how demand from India (and China, of course) would drive global energy prices in the years ahead. The debate seemed to have changed in a subtle yet significant manner: it was not about how oil prices would affect India but how India would affect oil prices. Around this time, I was writing an article on India and the third oil shock. Many of the research reports that I read hovered around the same point. Ed Yardeni, chief economist of Prudential Financial wrote: "In the long run, I seriously doubt that there is enough oil on planet earth to meet the needs of all of us driving SUVs, not just in America but also in India and China." A report by HSBC's global equities strategy team echoed Yardeni when it reminded investors of a few earlier reports where "we put forward the notion that higher oil prices were mainly a function of growing demand — particularly in India, China and other parts of developing Asia."[7]

India's high-octane economy is bound to guzzle oil in the coming decades. The standard response has been to go on a global hunt for oil supplies. The quest for "energy security" has taken the government oil companies into Asia and Africa — including badlands like Somalia and some of the former Soviet republics. There is a renewed drive to use more coal as well as some loose talk about promoting new sources of energy, like wind and solar power. And there are grand strategies to pipe natural gas into India, the most controversial of which is the plan to get gas from Iran. The hunt for oil and gas has excited both the politicians and the press, what with the mix of oil, politics, and foreign policy. The quest for energy security has attracted attention because, in a way, it is a dramatic reenactment of the 19th century Great Game, when Britain and Russia fought for supremacy in Afghanistan and the now oil-rich regions surrounding it.

While there is some justification for the global quest for energy supplies, the demand side has been completely ignored. There is little talk in India of how to use energy with greater efficiency. The International Energy Agency (IEA) calculates what it calls the energy-intensity of an economy. This is the amount of energy needed to produce one unit of GDP. It shows how well a country uses its energy supplies. In 2002, says the IEA, India had one of the most energy-intensive economies in the world — 2.88 times that of the rich countries.[8] So India needed nearly three times more than an average rich country to produce an equivalent amount of output (and there are no indications that things have changed since then). This is scandalous.

Generally, the rich countries use less oil per unit of output than the developing countries. This is because of a variety of reasons: better capital stock and modern infrastructure, for example. But the fact that rich countries have moved away from manufacturing also helps them conserve energy. And this is where India's energy-inefficient ways stand out. China, whose economy is powered by manufacturing, is less energy-intensive than India. India's energy intensity is almost 24% higher than China's, despite the fact that both countries are at the same level of development.

One way to keep India's dependence on imported oil down is to use energy more efficiently. The official India Hydrocarbon Vision 2025 report, for example, says that oil elasticity with respect to GDP is currently around 1.1. What does this mean? It means that India needs 1.1 extra units of oil to produce one extra unit of GDP. It was two in the 1970s and 1.2 in the 1980s. So the amount of oil used to power further economic growth has dropped over recent decades. The vision report expects oil elasticity to fall to 0.7 in 2025.[9]

Will this happen? It did happen in the rich countries. For the OECD as a whole, energy consumption per unit of output has fallen by around 25% since 1973, the year oil prices first shot up. Take one small country: Austria. Its energy consumption in 1992 was the same as it was in 1973, though industrial output was up 70%. Denmark is another country that has successfully de-linked energy consumption and economic growth. High taxes on heating oil and electricity for homes helped. In Japan, one major reason was the shift from heavy industries such as iron and steel to machine-based and high-tech ones like automobiles and consumer electronics.

The point is that there are lots of things to be done — from better infrastructure to higher taxes. The task of securing sources of oil in places like Sudan is the relatively simple job. It is a matter of diplomacy and investment. Cutting energy usage to more sensible levels will be far more difficult — which is perhaps why there is so little discussion about it in India. As India's economy guzzles energy, its sensitivity to shocks will increase over the years, unless it learns from countries like Japan and starts using energy more frugally.

JOBS FOR THE BOYS AND GIRLS

I have written earlier how poverty in India is often not a result of unemployment but of unproductive employment. The largest proportion of people who labor all day without earning adequate incomes live in the rural areas. Agriculture accounts for barely a quarter of the Indian economy but employs about 60% of the labor force. It means that six out of every 10 Indians are stuck in a sector that has been ignored by policy makers, starved of capital and has thus stagnated over the past few decades. What is the way out?

Some changes are already evident in the rural economy. It can no longer be blindly equated with the agricultural economy. Economist Omkar Goswami and marketing consultant Rama Bijapurkar have constructed a detailed representation of rural

India based on economic, demographic and consumption data from 530 districts in the country. They say that rural India accounts for 52% of India's GDP. They break this into the three basic components: agriculture accounts for 46%, industry for 21%, and services for 33% of the rural economy. So a moribund agricultural sector does not necessarily mean a dead-end rural economy. In a newspaper article, Goswami and Bijapurkar give one indication: the 1991 census showed that only 30% of rural households lived in permanent houses. Ten years later, the next census shows that 41% of rural households have decent housing.[10] This fact does not quite fit in with the politically attractive view that the whole of rural India is suffering because of problems on the farm.

That still leaves the issue of poverty and unproductive employment. It is clear that agriculture cannot absorb more people. There are some initial signs that labor is moving out into other parts of the economy. Rural industry and services may have absorbed some of the excess labor released from the farm. A new round of reforms in agriculture could help the process.

The challenge can be framed in a simple manner. India's near-tryst with mass starvation after the droughts of the late 1960s made successive governments paranoid about food security. Farm policy since then has focused almost entirely on cereal production. India now produces more rice and wheat than it needs. The government-owned Food Corporation of India has often run out of places to store the mountains of excess cereals it buys. Grain is often left in the open, where it is destroyed by rains and eaten by rats.

Meanwhile, consumption patterns have changed with rising prosperity. Indians consume more milk, fruit, vegetables, eggs, and meat that before. The importance of cereals has diminished. Demand has changed but supply has not. One of the major tasks before Indian farmers is to align their production with the new patterns of food consumption. But stuff such as milk and meat is perishable. It needs to be brought to market efficiently and quickly. Or it has to be processed in order to have a longer shelf life. This needs a lot of things — better rural roads, cold chains, fleets of trucks, and processing plants. The employment potential in support industries and services can be immense (one truck company has calculated that the sale of one truck creates a dozen secondary jobs, for drivers, mechanics, loaders, etc.).

One of the troubling misconceptions in India is that only large-scale industry can create jobs. Few seem to care than manufacturing continues to shed jobs the world over, as labor productivity increases by leaps and bounds in factories. The mainstream view is that India has had jobless growth in recent years. That is not quite true, but the ability of the Indian economy to create new jobs has undoubtedly diminished in the past 15 years. One unit of economic growth created 0.384 jobs in the 1980s and 0.312 jobs in the 1990s, according to estimates by Ifzal Ali, chief economist of the Asian Development Bank.[11] If one assumes that the employment elasticity of economic growth has been unchanged in recent years (or, in other words, one unit of economic growth still generates the same units of employment that it did in the 1990s) then a long-term growth rate of 7.5% a year should lead to a 2.34% growth in employment. India's labor force is currently growing at less than 2% a year. This means that the incremental demand for labor could be outstripping the growth in the supply of labor, which is perhaps why wages for some types of work are rising.

Critics like to argue that the wrong jobs are being created in India — in the informal sector and in low-end services. It is the world of the truck driver, the maid and the security guard. The great Indian working class deserves better. To many economists and policy makers at different ends of the ideological spectrum, industrial employment offers great hope. It is assumed that it will draw workers away from the informal sector and also absorb the excess millions who are stuck in agriculture. The proposition is an attractive one, but is also deeply flawed.

Let us compare India and China. As is well known, economic growth in China has been heavily dependent on industrial production. Giant factories along its coastal belt have become the global hub for low-cost production, spewing out everything from cotton textiles to computer chips at rock-bottom prices. Factories in the Pearl River Delta region boast far higher levels of labor productivity than those in India. Should India replicate the Chinese strategy?

Few people realize that China's employment intensity is very low, almost embarrassingly so. In the 1990s, when China's FDI-led strategy of industrial growth came into its own, the employment elasticity of growth in that country was down to a mere 0.129, compared to India's more healthy 0.312. India generates 2.5 times more jobs per unit of economic growth than China does. Two factors have helped China keep ahead in its huge battle against mass unemployment. First, economic growth has been in excess of 10% a year through most of the past quarter century. Second, China's population growth has declined. Even so, the communist party bosses are often spooked by the spectre of mass unemployment and social instability. That is what keeps them pressing the accelerator when it seems more prudent to apply the brakes.

India cannot depend on manufacturing for its jobs. Its economy is growing slower than China's while the labor force is growing more rapidly. It is widely agreed that India needs to create 10 to 15 million new jobs every year. There is no need to scoff at the low-end jobs that are likely to be created in both the urban and rural areas. The alternative could be social instability.

The threats are quite real. The Asian Development Bank website quoted the bank's chief economist Ifzal Ali's grim warning when he was speaking on the bank's new report on labor markets in India:

> "The outlines of an Asian employment crisis are already taking shape. Strong economic growth alone will not solve the problem. Even in countries that have achieved relatively high growth rates of output, employment growth has been disappointing. Governments must focus on providing full, productive, and decent employment for their people if their economies are to provide equitable growth and development."[12]

THE LONG AND WINDING (AND POTHOLED) ROAD

In the last weeks of 2004, motorists driving out of Mumbai for a year-end escape from the urban crush could not have failed to notice a snaking wall of trucks on both sides of the highway leading out of the city. The trucks carried containers stocked with goods headed for foreign markets. The economy had started revving up after three years of sluggish growth. Foreign trade was benefiting. The modern Jawaharlal Nehru Port, which lies on the other side of Mumbai harbor and is India's biggest and most efficient port, could not handle the pressure. It was taking weeks before containers headed for foreign markets could be loaded onto the waiting ships. Exporters could not meet delivery schedules. Domestic manufacturers had to stock up on inventory to avoid production delays because of the late arrival of imported inputs. It was unofficially estimated that India lost about a billion dollars of foreign trade that year because of the logjam in its ports.

The story repeats itself with unerring and depressing regularity. India's tattered infrastructure is an embarrassment. Trucks and buses crawl along national and state highways at an average speed of 25 kph, half the global average. The magnificent Changi airport at Singapore handles more passenger and freight traffic than all the airports in India put together do. The average turnaround time for a ship in an Indian port has halved over the past decade, from seven days to about 3.5 days. Yet, the improved turnaround time is leagues away from what happens in the world's major ports like Rotterdam, where an average ship is turned around in a matter of hours.[13] Power shortages are endemic. The results of poor infrastructure are lost export orders, high inventory costs, additional capital costs for captive power generation and much more. It is as if Indian industry has to rattle along dirt tracks while its global competitors coast along smooth Formula One tracks.

The appalling infrastructure deficit does not hurt industry alone. There is no rural infrastructure to speak of. I have visited regions in Maharashtra, one of the country's richest states, where there were 14-hour power cuts in the villages during the summer of 2005. Large private companies have the financial muscle to invest in their own backup power generation units. But what can farmers and owners of small rural workshops do? Rural roads often exist only on maps, rather than on the ground, where they have disintegrated into potholed horrors. What is worse, 52% of India's rural population cannot access whatever passes off for a rural road network.

The ability to access markets, get better prices and improve productivity is seriously hampered by the lack of proper infrastructure. For example, Cesar Calderon of the Central Bank of Chile and Luis Serven of the World Bank show that Latin American economies would benefit greatly if they bring their infrastructure to the level of Costa Rica's. Long-term economic growth would rise by between 1.1% and 4.8% a year while the Gini coefficient (a measure of inequality) would drop by between 0.12% and 0.10%.[14] It is not just about economics, however. Universal access to high-quality infrastructure is a must in a democratic society.

Ironically, India started off with one of the best infrastructure networks in Asia. The British Empire needed railways and roads to move troops and raw materials around the subcontinent. Private investment in the railways was encouraged by the colonial government, which gave a guarantee that investors would earn 5% a year on their money. India did not see any direct fighting during the Second World War, unlike the rest of Asia. So its stock of physical infrastructure was untouched by bombs and destruction. Yet, 60 years later, India has perhaps the worst infrastructure in the whole of Asia.

Most Asian countries have spent around 7% of their national incomes every year on building infrastructure. India currently spends just 3.5% of its national income on roads, ports, railways, airports, etc. This means that it will have to double its infrastructure spending over the next few years if it is to start catching up with the rest of Asia — half the money will be needed to build new infrastructure and the other half to maintain existing facilities. Though the national savings rate is climbing, it is difficult to believe that all this money can be sucked from the domestic savings pool. Foreign investment too will be necessary. Prime Minister Manmohan Singh has repeatedly said that India would need $150 billion of foreign investment in infrastructure over the next decade.

We have seen the first attempts to bridge the infrastructure deficit. Telecom has been a clear winner, with the number of telephones per thousand Indians increasing 10 times over 10 years. Road construction too has picked up, especially after former Prime Minister Atal Bihari Vajpayee pushed through the Golden Quadrilateral Project, with its innovative funding and exemplary execution. Yet, according to a report published by investment bank Morgan Stanley, China spent $260 billion on electricity, construction, transportation, telecom, and real estate. India spent $31 billion that year. The Golden Quadrilateral is estimated to cost $12 billion over eight years. China spends twice that amount every year on new roads.

In short, it's a Himalayan task. The government cannot do the job on its own, which is not necessarily a bad thing given the fact that it was government inaction that left India with such poor infrastructure in the first place. Private investment is needed. The challenge then is putting the right sort of incentives and regulations in place. Private investment in telecom faltered between 1994 and 1999 because of a huge regulatory mess. A historic settlement between the government and the private telecom companies — the main element of which was a move from fixed license fees to a revenue sharing arrangement — was the turning point. Similar progress is needed in roads, ports, and power. Successive governments over the past five years have made honest attempts to get ahead with the job.

The infrastructure problem is a bit of a chicken and egg situation. What comes first? Countries cannot grow rich without high-quality infrastructure and the money for this infrastructure cannot be raised unless there is wealth generated in an economy. The government of the day has to take the risk and build infrastructure that is far better than what is required immediately. Singapore built Changi airport more than two decades ago. The airport not only served current needs, but also helped the city-state emerge as a business and tourism hub for Asia. It is easy to scoff at China's investment mania and its empty six-lane highways that lead nowhere. The point is that these highways will be there even 30 years from now, well after the investment bubble has popped; they will, then, be servicing the needs of a bigger Chinese economy.

India's quest for providing its citizens with good roads, clean drinking water, and uninterrupted power has just begun. There is a long and tortuous road ahead.

NOTES

1. There has been a lot of debate on the poverty trend in recent years. Some of the best articles on this contentious issue have been collected in a very fine book, *The Great Indian Poverty Debate*, edited by Angus Deaton and Valerie Kozel; Macmillan India (2005).
2. See *Forbes Asia*, March 27, 2006.
3. "Capital ideas", by Avinash Celestine, *Business World*, March 6, 2006.
4. "Have reforms failed the poor", by Niranjan Rajadhyaksha, *Business World*, June 21, 2004.
5. In an interview with the author.
6. Some of the data here has been taken from *Reliance Review of Energy Markets*, compiled by the Energy Research Group at Reliance Industries (August 2003).
7. "Investment strategy weekly", by Ed Yardeni, Prudential Equity Group, August 16, 2004, *Equities And Oil Deficiency: Energy Deficiency*? HSBC, August 20, 2004.

8. "Analysis of the Impact of High Oil Prices on the Global Economy", International Energy Agency (May 2004).

9. Hydrocarbon Vision 2025 Report, Ministry Of Petroleum & Natural Gas, Government of India (2001). Available at: http://www.petrowatch.com/government.html.

10. "India Is Not Just About Agriculture", by Omkar Goswami and Rama Bijapurkar, *Business Standard*, July 16, 2005. They were replying to an article published earlier in the same newspaper by Abheek Barua titled "The 1.9% growth economy."

11. See "Labour Markets in Asia: Issues and Perspectives", Asian Development Bank (2005), available at: http://www.adb.org.

12. Available at: http://www.adb.org/media/Articles/2006/9757-Asia-job-creation/.

13. "The long and winding road, a survey of Indian infrastructure", by Supriya Kurane, *Business World*, January 31, 2005.

14. ibid.

Epilogue

There are clear signs in the middle of the first decade of the 21st century that India is on a new and higher growth path. The fastest sustained growth the Indian economy has ever seen till now was in the three years between 1994–1995 and 1996–1997, when the economy grew at over 7% for three years in a row and at an average rate of 7.47%. The figures for the three years since 2003–2004 have seen an even higher average growth rate of 8.1%. Furthermore, in the summer of 2006, at the time of writing these words, most economists were forecasting at least another two years of growth in excess of 7%. In short, India is in the midst of an unprecedented economic boom.

Will it last? Every sunny story has its dark corners, and the Indian economy in the middle of the first decade of this century is not without significant risks, many of which have been mentioned in earlier chapters. Yet there is reason to believe that India is very likely to stay on a high-growth path over the next decade or two. The current growth acceleration can be ascribed to a combination of cyclical and structural factors. It is the structural factors that will help keep the Indian economy on a high-growth path despite the ups and downs of the economic cycles. This book has dealt with the six structural factors that matter in the long run.

India is today saving and investing like never before. Part of the reason for the higher savings rate is the demographic change and the beginning of a two-decade bulge in the working age population. Both the investment rate and the labor force are increasing. What this means in very simple terms is that India is now putting more labor and capital to the task of economic development. Efficiency levels in some parts of the economy have already improved because of market reforms and globalization. Better infrastructure will only lead to further efficiency gains as well as help couple large swathes of the country's economy with the global economy. More capital accumulation, a bigger labor force and better efficiency should lead to better economic performance. It normally does.

Two key challenges have to be met: capital should not be frittered away in the wrong sort of projects, and the ability of the economy to absorb higher levels of savings and investment should be improved. That, in turn, will require a more inclusive financial system and more economic reforms (especially in certain areas like agriculture). I have tried to show in this book that it is the poor of this country who bear the brunt of the failure to increase financial access and free the economy further. The poor do not have adequate access to modern finance and they often find themselves tied down with restrictions that the corporate sector has long been released from. It is precisely to remedy this situation that it is imperative to push through more reforms.

So, while India is already reporting far better economic performance than it ever did, it still has a long way to go. Look at Table 9 below. It shows how fast other Asian economies grew during their growth accelerations. India needs to do more.

Table 9
Growth Accelerations

Country	Period	Average growth rate (%)
India	1990–2000	6.0
India	2000–2005	6.4
China	1994–2004	9.7–10.4*
Hong Kong	1960–1995	7.7
Korea	1960–1995	8.1
Singapore	1960–1995	8.4
Taiwan	1960–1995	8.6
Thailand	1960–1995	7.5
Malaysia	1960–1995	6.9
Japan	1950–1980	8.0

Source: UBS Investment Research.
*Note: China is in a range because it reflects incomplete national income data following a statistical revision done in early 2006.

The point is that it is pretty easy for economists to make growth assumptions. India can grow at 8% a year if its investment rate climbs to 32% of GDP and its capital efficiency is unchanged; and an investment rate of 40% will yield a 10% growth rate. But is that all? Economic growth is eventually the sum of the actions of companies, farmers, traders, consumers, and the like — in other words, of ordinary people and their organizations. They will do a better job only if they have greater economic freedom. The core issue then is not how high the investment rate and other macroeconomic aggregates can go, but how much more of an open economy India can become in the coming years.

AN OPEN ECONOMY AND AN OPEN SOCIETY

Independent India has been a curious combination of an open society and a closed economy, and embedded in this arrangement was the implicit assumption that ordinary people were intelligent enough to choose their rulers but not intelligent enough to choose what to buy and produce. The combination is curious for another reason as well: open economies have tended to be open societies, and vice versa. There have also been a few rare cases where free economies have been implanted on repressed societies: Chile during the reign of the military junta in the 1970s and 1980s and contemporary China are two examples of countries where bazaars and bayonets have coexisted in an uneasy truce. But India is perhaps unique in the way it has combined a free society with a fettered economy.

Political freedom has helped the silent majority in India make its voice heard. It has also been a wonderful vehicle of social mobility and one reason why the old social hierarchies were shattered after Independence. The lack of economic freedom, however, ensured that the aspirations that were unleashed by political freedom could not be adequately met in a moribund economy. One way to look at the economic changes since 1991 is by reinterpreting the reforms in a slightly broader context than is usual. They are the first steps in the long journey toward an open society and an open economy, where both political and economic freedoms coexist. The journey has been exciting, productive — and incomplete. For example, India is still technically a socialist society where the right to property is not recognized as a fundamental right. (India was, of course, *not* technically a socialist society and the right to property was very much recognized as a fundamental right by the Constitution when it was adopted in 1950. India was formally declared "socialist" by the Forty-second Amendment pushed through Parliament in 1976, at the height of the Emergency. Later, quite inexplicably, the fundamental right to property was obliterated from the Constitution by the Forty-fourth Amendment under the post-Emergency Janata Government.)

The government and its bureaucracy can (and do) come in the way of the natural human inclination to truck, barter, and trade with unerring regularity.

Despite the great advances made over the past two decades or so, markets are still not allowed to function in many parts of the Indian economy. In fact, the poor often have to face a licensing regime that is as repressive as the one that organized industry faced till 1991. The writer Fareed Zakaria has given us the concept of an illiberal democracy — a country where elections and the other paraphernalia of democracy exist but where a writer can be lynched for his views. India sometimes tends to be the economic variant of an illiberal democracy, in the sense that the reforms at the top do not adequately translate into economic freedoms on the street. The single biggest challenge for the country in the coming years is not building better roads or boosting exports; it is giving every citizen the advantage of property rights and functioning markets.

At the same time, it would also be wrong to take an open society for granted. There has been a tide of cultural nationalism in India (partly as a reaction to militant Islamic fundamentalism) that often leads to extreme intolerance. This constitutes a potential push toward a closed society. India's deep tradition of religious and cultural tolerance is a strong defense against such tendencies, but an open economy can do its bit as well to keep intolerance at bay.

The Bharatiya Janata Party (BJP), which is positioned to appeal to the growing sense of the "Hindu angst," had to come to terms with a dilemma when it headed a coalition government from 1998 to 2004. It had to choose between cultural nationalism and liberal economics. "The Hindu nationalist project hides a profound paradox: the maintenance of traditional identity demands material strength but the means to that strength are likely to undercut traditional identity," writes political scientist Baldev Raj Nayar.[1]

The BJP eventually chose liberal economics over cultural conservatism, at least in some measure. There are some signs that a part of the Left too now realizes that a free economy is a powerful tool for change. While the party hacks continue to rail against what they see as a sell-out to imperialist forces, those who run governments on behalf of the Left parties waste no time in wooing foreign investment. The Left too, in its own way, is being forced to grapple with a variant of the dilemma that the BJP has grappled with. The success of the open economy has forced its natural opponents to rethink their positions.

Manmohan Singh, the architect of India's economic reforms and now its prime minister, wrote recently:

> "A nation is empowered by its people. A people are empowered by their capabilities. People's capabilities are created by investments in their education, well-being and skills and [by] providing them with opportunities for gainful productive employment. People are also empowered by the freedom they enjoy.... Open societies enable the full flowering of our individual personality. Open economies provide the space for the fruition of our creativity and enterprise. Open societies and open economies empower those who live and work in them. Being an open democratic society and an open economy empowers India. Provision of effective social safety nets for the weak and needy will ensure that all sections of our population will participate in [the] processes of social and economic growth, making for a more inclusive society."[2]

India's transition to an open economy and an open society has begun in earnest. It is not just about changes at the top. What I have tried to examine in this book is how the revolutions in economics, demographics, trade, technology, and society are empowering ordinary Indians with the freedom to make choices about how to work, consume, and invest. The economic reforms of 1991 were like the first drop of ink on a sheet of blotting paper; with the passage of time, the stain has spread wide and far. This book has tried to explain that spreading stain rather than the drops from above. The changes we are seeing in India will become far more difficult to reverse as the stain spreads over a still wider area.

Meanwhile, India's dramatic transformation is being played out in full view of the rest of the world. The immediate global interest in India is, naturally, because of the commercial opportunities it offers in terms of consumer markets, technological capabilities, stock market investments, and the like. But, quite apart from the interests of corporate bosses, venture capitalists, and portfolio managers, there is another reason why the rest of the world would be well advised to keep a close eye on India.

One of the grand debates in 20th century economics was whether a country could make its initial assault on poverty with a democratic political system. Or does it take a dictatorship to manage the primitive accumulation of capital? If India wins its battle against mass poverty over the next two decades while maintaining both an open economy and an open society, the big question should be settled once and for all. Yes, it is possible for democracies to develop. What India is doing right now has never been attempted before in the annals of human history — an attempt to combine political democracy with early-stage economic development. The likely success of this experiment could provide a working model for other poor countries in the 21st century.

NOTES

1. "The Limits of Economic Nationalism In India: Economic Reforms Under The BJP-Led Government", 1998–99, by Baldev Raj Nayar (2000), available at: http://www.nd.edu/~kellogg/pdfs/Nayar.pdf.
2. "Open Democracy and Open Economy", an article published in *The Indian Express*, August 15, 2005. Also available at: http://www.indiaempowered.com.

Index

A

Ali, Ifzal, 161, 162

B

Banerjee, Abhijit, 117
Bangalored, 11
Bank computerization, 76
Bank nationalization, 108 110
Bauer, Peter, 5, 38
Bhagwati, Jagdish, 12, 39
Bhalla, Surjit, 153
Bharat Forge, 88–89
Bijapurkar, Rama, 159, 160
Billionaries, Forbes listing, 154
Bombay Club, 92
Bombay, cotton boom, 33
Bombay, early dissenters, 39–40
Brahmananda, P.R., 35–39
Brar, D.S., 86
Bubble, benefits of, 77
Buenos Aires, 139
Bunti Aur Babli, 124

C

Chandra, Bipan, 36
Chavan, Madhav, 58
China and India, 20–23, 161
China, aging, 63–64
Computer, first in India, 71
Consumption pattern
  changing, 160

Convergence, 43, 45
Cost disease, 70

D

Das, Gurcharan, 91
De Soto, Hernando, 139
Deaton, Angus, 153
Debroy, Vivek, 133–134
Demographic dividend, 64
Dcsai, Meghnad, 35
Development, defined as
  greater choice, 5
Dil Chahta Hai, 123
Distributed production and
  globalization, 94
Dobbs, Lou, 12, 13, 14
Doing Business In India,
  World Bank report, 143–144
Drain theory, 35
Dreze, Jean, 153
Drought in India, 18
Dubey, Satyendra, 128
Duflo, Esther, 117

E

Early nationalists and their
  views on foreign trade, 36
Economic reform, three
  waves, 135–136
Economic triage, 18
Education, fundamental
  right, 56

Employment elasticity of growth, 161
Equity bubble, 8

F

Farmer suicides, 153
Feenstra, Robert C., 94
Financial depth, 104, 112
Financial health, 104
Financial sector reform debate, 106–108
Fishermen, using GPS, 146
Flying geese, 17
Friedman, Milton, 38–39

G

Gadgil, D.R., 33
Gandhi, Rajiv, 75
Gaurav, Kumar, 141, 142
Global supply chains and trade, 95
Globalisation index, Foreign Policy and A.T. Kerany, 98
Goldman Sachs, 24
Goswami, Omkar, 159, 160
Green Revolution, 19
Growth accelerations, 168
Gupta, Shekhar, 123

H

Handicrafts and global markets, 147–148

I

IBM exit from India, 74
ICICI Bank, 118–120
IIT effect, 126–128

India and first wave of globalisation, 32
India, contribution to Asia growth, 99
India, contribution to global growth, 99
India, demographic sweet spot, 53
India, energy-intensity, 158
India, high tariffs, 100
India, infrastructure, 20, 162–165
India, Malthusian fears, 18, 50
India, savings rate increases, 103
India, share of global trade, 98
India, share of world economy (1500–2000), 3
India, starts to reclaim its lost position, 2
Indian companies, nature of global acquisitions, 91
Indian industry, early days, 34
Inequality, 154
Infosys Technologies, 74
iPod, 14

J

Japan, aging, 63
Japan, Meiji Restoration, 29
Japan, response to energy shock, 159
Jha Raghbendra, 138, 153, 156, 160

K

Kaldor, Nicholas, 155

Kamath, K.V., 118–119
Kelkar, Vijay, 24
Kerry, John, 12
Kohli, F.C., 73
Kota, coaching factories,
  126–128
Krishnamurthi, J., 7
Krugman, Paul, 94
Kuznets curve, 154
Kuznets, Simon, 154

L

Lal, Deepak, 36
Lalita Kumari, 57–58
Lazy banking, 116–117
Lee Kuan Yew, 80, 130
Legal system, 133
Leonard, Andrew, 14
License-permit raj, 37
Liebl, Maureen, 147
Loan melas, 114–115

M

Maddison, Angus, 43
Mahbubani, Kishore, 23
Mankiw, N. Gregory, 12
Manmohan Singh, 41, 171
Mann, Catherine, 81
Maoists, 8, 156
Mid-day meal program, 60
Middle path, 47
Moffet, Matt, 139
Moynihan, Daniel Patrick, 1
Myrdal, Gunnar, 18, 19

N

Nayar, Baldev Raj, 170

Nehru, Jawaharlal, flawed
  vision, 37
New Delhi consensus, 46
Nilekani, Nandan, 96
North Korea, 16

O

Oil shocks, 157
Open economy, 169
Open society, 169
Outsourcing, as a new form
  of international trade, 81
Outsourcing, as a new form
  of trade, 12
Outsourcing, beneficiaries, 68
Outsourcing, critics in India, 83

P

Paddock, William and Paul, 18
Paithan, artisans, 148
Panagriya, Arvind, 156
Pawar, Sharad, 18
Popper, Karl, 7
Population and savings, 53–54
Poverty and productivity, 134
Poverty rates, 153
Priceless planning, 38
Private schools, 128–130
Project Bhoomi, 145–146
Project Drishtee, 146
Property and prosperity,
  138–143
Property rights, need for
  clear, 140

R

Railway porters, restrictions
  on, 141

Rajagopalachari, C., 37
Rajan, Raghuram, 15
Ranbaxy Laboratories, 85
Rangarajan, C., 76
Reforms, early, 45
Ricardo, David, 81
Rice trade, restrictions on, 138
Robinson, Joan, 16
Roy, Tirthankar, 147
Roychand, Premchand, 32
Rubin, Robert, 97

S

Samuelson, Paul, 13
School enrollments rising, 57
School teachers, truancy, 58–60
Sen, Abhijit, 155
Shenoy, B.R., 40
Ship-to-mouth economy, 18
Significance of debate, 15
Singhal, Mayank, 141, 142
Smith, Adam, 4
Social attitudes, change, 122

Spending patterns, 125

T

Talwar, R.K., 115
Tata, Jamshetji, 30
Texas Instruments, first earth
    station, 75
Tooley, James, 131
Tourism deficit, 130
Twin crises, 108

V

Vakil, C.N., 39
Vivekananda, 30

W

Waslekar, Sundeep, 156
White, William, 137

Y

Yardeni, Ed, 157